ROTHERHAM PUBLIC LIBRARIES

Portrait of a Decade

The 1940s

NANCE LUI FYSON

B.T. Batsford Ltd, London

Contents

© Nance Lui Fyson 1988
First published 1988

Typeset by Tek-Art Ltd Kent
and printed and bound
in Great Britain by
Richard Clay Ltd
Chichester, Sussex
for the publishers
B.T. Batsford Ltd
4 Fitzhardinge Street
London W1H 0AH

ISBN 0 7134 5628 0

Introduction

'Don't you know there's a war on?' This key phrase was behind much of what happened during the 1940s. The Second World War dominated events up to 1945, and the effects were felt for years after as well. Rationing, shortages, separation of families and homelessness were facts of life for millions of people in Britain. There were bombs, black-outs, evacuations and endless entreaties to save and 'make do'. 'Is your journey really necessary?' was a typical UK government poster.

The time of conflict was followed by a coming together of nations. The United Nations was born out of world confrontation and the desire for such chaos never to happen again. Countries began to see themselves as linked in a global order. New UN agencies began dealing with the after-effects of war, and have continued dealing with world problems ever since.

Despite the hopes for worldwide peace after the war, new divisions did develop. The Cold War between Russia and the Western nations began, as did the arms race. Opposition to the fascism of Nazi Germany was replaced by fears of the spread of communism.

Colonies were seeking independence, and a number of new nations came into being in the late 1940s. These included India, Pakistan, Burma, Ceylon, Indonesia and Israel. As some old groupings were broken, other units were formed. NATO (the North Atlantic Treaty Organisation) included the United States and 11 European countries in a pact of mutual defence. GATT (a General Agreement on Tariffs and Trade) included 23 countries who agreed to reduce barriers to world trade.

While the 1940s was a serious and even grim decade in many ways, it had its lively and enjoyable aspects, too. It was the age of the 'big bands', and dancing was a favourite escape from the harsh realities of the war. Songs with uplifting titles like 'We'll Meet Again' and 'Powder Your Nose with Sunshine' filled the hit parade. Films were another popular diversion, and cinema attendance soared. Stars such as Bing Crosby, Humphrey Bogart and Betty Grable were favourites. Artists and writers continued their work, and many were inspired by the decade's dramatic upheavals. The existentialist philosophy of Albert Camus and Jean-Paul Sartre as well as George Orwell's novel *1984* reflected dismay at the 'condition of man'.

Music flourished – from Charlie Parker's 'bebop' jazz to serious composers like Ralph Vaughan Williams and Benjamin Britten. Playwrights like Tennessee Williams, Noël Coward and Eugene O'Neill produced some of their most famous productions. Important novelists of the decade included W. Somerset Maugham, Graham Greene and Evelyn Waugh. Other famous artists included poets like T.S. Eliot, the sculptor Barbara Hepworth and the painters Francis Bacon and Jackson Pollock.

Television broadcasts had begun in 1936, but it was only after the war that they slowly became widespread. Radio was all-important during the war years. The BBC broadcast in 46 different languages (including overseas). It transmitted vital news and radio speeches, such as those by Churchill, Britain's wartime prime minister, to keep up the British morale. There was also William Joyce ('Lord Haw-Haw') who broadcast from Germany trying to spread rumours and depress listeners in Britain. (He was hanged after the war for treason.) The morale of homesick American GIs in the Pacific War was being undermined by 'Tokyo Rose', who hinted that wives and girlfriends might not stay faithful. The Armed Forces' Radio Service

Wartime posters: (top) in Britain people were being encouraged to grow more vegetables; (below) in Germany, women were told 'you too can help'.

Introduction

countered this with broadcasts by 'GI Jill'. Radio was also used to send coded messages to resistance movements.

Entertainment on radio was important as well. BBC's 'Transatlantic Quiz' started in 1944, bringing together American and British pundits. In the 'Brains Trust' (from 1941 to 1948), a panel of experts answered questions from listeners. 'The Goldbergs' were a favourite family serial comedy in America until 1945 (and then again on television from 1948). 'ITMA' ('It's That Man Again'), with Tommy Handley, was a regular comedy favourite in Britain. 'Dick Barton, Special Agent' was another serial, especially popular with children. 'The Archers' began in 1949.

Popular music underwent a change, as lead singers became featured. There were Vera Lynn, Dinah Shore, Frank Sinatra ('King of Swoon') and many others. Musicals became popular, starting with 'Oklahoma!', which opened in New York in 1943.

After the austerity of the war years fashion changed markedly in the late 1940s. The 'New Look' used fabric more freely and made women look more feminine. 'Zoot suits' were a 1940s' fashion for men, with large, long jackets and a hanging chain to be swung from the hips.

Sports were much reduced during the war. Grounds in the UK were often used by the army or planted with vegetables. In the USA, the Lawn Tennis Association resolved to carry on. Tournaments raised funds for the American Red Cross and other war efforts. As peace returned, there was more time and energy for sporting activities. More golfers and footballers turned professional. Some of the sporting stars who emerged were American baseball's Joe Di Maggio, the wrestler 'Gorgeous George' and British cricket's Denis Compton.

The world conflict prompted advances in science and technology – from chipboard to faster, safer aircraft and atomic power. Shortage of steel encouraged the use of more pre-stressed concrete in architecture. Other developments ranged from the first electronic computers to terylene, the ball-point pen, DDT, fluorescent lighting, aerosols, polaroid cameras, transistors, automated assembly, microwave ovens and disposable nappies (diapers).

There were many social changes in the decade as well. The war brought more women out of the home and into the world of paid work. Sexual morals became less strict, encouraged by the uncertainties of war. Even child-rearing was changing. Dr Spock's *Common Sense Book of Baby and Child Care*, published in 1946, prompted a much freer and more child-centred approach.

The 1940s was also a time of new beginnings. The whole world of the 'teenager' was born in wartime America and came to Britain just after. The term 'juvenile delinquency' came across the Atlantic as well. By the end of the decade the era of the 'drive-in' had begun in the USA, with many cinemas opening. Package tours had a modest start in 1947, as air travel generally expanded. (In 1946 American scheduled airlines carried ten times more passengers than they had done in 1938.)

By the end of the decade, the effects of war were fading. 'Bigger newspapers again!' was the headline in 1949 as newspapers in Britain

The grim reality of war: a German sentry patrols the Atlantic Wall.

Peace was declared in Europe in May 1945, but Japan refused to surrender until August, when two atomic bombs were dropped on the cities of Hiroshima and Nagasaki, killing some 250,000 people.

Introduction

increased from four pages to six. Many peoples' lives were shattered by the war, but it was also a decade of heightened values. People learned important lessons about what was most important in life – and how to endlessly 'make-do' with less.

AH ! CRIPPSO !

This newspaper cartoon by Strube in 1948 was a parody of a Bisto advertisement. The whiff of better things to come was meant to console people. Britain was still under the austerity measures of Stafford Cripps (Chancellor of the Exchequer).

Britain is

The *real* war begins

GERMANY'S INVASION OF POLAND on 1 September 1939 marked the beginning. Britain and France declared war on Germany two days later. The Second World War was already underway when the new decade began, but it was still being called the 'phoney war'. The real conflicts did not start until the spring of 1940.

Battle of Britain

IT WAS NOT UNTIL JULY that the German leader, Adolf Hitler, even considered invading Britain. The German air force, called the Luftwaffe, began air attacks. The intention was to destroy the British air force, so that a German invasion of Britain would be possible.

In August, the Luftwaffe attacked Royal Air Force stations around London. By mistake, some planes dropped bombs on London itself. This led to 80 British bombers being sent to bomb Berlin the next night. More raids on London followed.

15 September became known as 'Battle of Britain Day'. One hundred and seventy planes clashed in battle over Kent. British Hurricanes and Spitfires tangled with German bombers. The victory for Britain was important. As the Prime Minister, Winston Churchill, said of the day: 'Never in the field of human conflict was so much owed by so many to so few.'

A series of attacks and battles over several months caused much damage, but the Royal Air Force showed its strength. The people of Britain were determined to resist. No invasion of Britain ever came.

Bombing raids

ATTACKS ON the British civilian population were stepped up from early September. These regular, heavy air attacks came to be known as the 'The Blitz' (from the German word *Blitzkrieg* meaning 'lightening war').

For nine months the Germans tried to destroy the morale of the British people. London was not the only city to be hit; Brighton, Southampton, Dover, Coventry and several others suffered as well.

Thousands fled the towns, 'trekking' to camp out in rural areas less likely to be hit. Shelters were also used. Curved shells of corrugated steel (Anderson shelters) were put up in some gardens. Many people spent uncomfortable nights in these. Others went to sleep in damp street shelters or in London's Underground. Many preferred to take their chances at home, sometimes sleeping in a cupboard under the stairs. Some people took refuge under strong steel tables called Morrison Shelters.

The Anderson shelter was made of curved corrugated iron and covered with earth. Many were distributed free to families at the start of the war.

bombed

Eyewitness accounts

LAST NIGHT and in the early hours of this morning we experienced our worst aerial bombardment. . . . Suddenly there came a whistle, shrill, followed by another nearer, yet a third, this time seemingly on top of us. Bombs! . . . . I was awakened almost hourly, and lay listening to the roar of jockeying planes, the scream of bombs, and the terrific noise of our guns which vibrated in my ears. I looked out – fires, search-lights, shells – a pandemonium.
Diary entry for 25 September 1940, quoted in Colin Perry, *Boy in the Blitz*, Leo Cooper Ltd, 1972

One of the biggest raids came on the night of 14 November. Some 400 bombs were dropped on Coventry. Nearly 1500 people died and thousands were made homeless.

Coventry has been the victim of the most concentrated, if not the worst raid since the war began.
I have just come back from the centre of the city. The cathedral is in ruins, except for the tower. Over a large area surrounding it there lies the stench of burning houses.
A few miles out of Coventry I saw the first large body of refugees walking along the roadside. Children were being carried in their fathers' arms and pushed along in perambulators. There were suitcases and bundles on peoples' shoulders. Little families trudged along with rugs, blankets and anything they could have saved from their ruined homes.
Daily Herald, 15 November 1940

On the evening of 29 December, the German Luftwaffe paid a two-hour visit over the City of London:

Two hours. That was all it took. In that time, 1400 fires were lit on the roof-tops of the City. The whole area between St Paul's and

13 June 1940. Evacuation of about 120,000 London schoolchildren began. Most of the children went to Cornwall, Devon, Somerset and Wales, where, it was thought, they would be safer.

the Guildhall was alight. Eight glorious Wren churches, the Guildhall, the Law Courts, the Tower of London were among the victims. In the streets men ran between buildings that were solid walls of fire. The air was filled with a blizzard of sparks. Right at the heart of the swirling clouds of smoke and flame, the great dome of St Paul's Cathedral stood while all around it perished. . . .
Daily Mail, 31 December 1940

Evacuation

OVER ONE AND A HALF MILLION British people (mainly children and mothers) had been moved out of cities and towns in September 1939. It was thought they would be safer in the countryside. By January 1940, over half had drifted home again, as the expected air attacks had not happened. Once bombing *did* start in 1940 the evacuations began again. In one week in June nearly 100,000 London children were sent to the West Country. Children were sent abroad as well. Thousands of children were 'seavacuated' to Canada, the USA and elsewhere.

7

Germans invade

AFTER TAKING Norway and Denmark in early 1940, the Germans invaded Holland and Belgium on 10 May. Masses of people began leaving Paris, as the occupation of France also looked likely.

Every road was completely blocked. Hundreds of cars had broken down or were out of petrol. Great columns of Parisians on foot added themselves to the lines of cars, lorries, carts, bicycles jammed along every exit road for hundreds of miles. It was mid-afternoon on Monday when we learned for certain that German tanks were across the Seine trying to cut off roads from the city to the south.
Daily Express, 11 May 1940

Wounded men evacuated at Dunkirk show good spirits at a south coast port.

Evacuation at Dunkirk: the fall of France

'A BLOODY MIRACLE' is what one newspaper called it. While French civilians walked south, soldiers of the British Expeditionary Force made their way to Dunkirk. From there they were brought back to Britain by the Royal Navy, helped by small boats and ordinary fishermen who had set out from ports all along the south coast of Britain. By 2 June, over 224,000 BEF men had been rescued. Another 95,000 troops, mainly French, were brought safely to Britain as well. About 2000 men were lost as ships and boats were sunk by Germans.

The tired, unwashed British soldiers were given a heroes' welcome – and the chance to fight another day. The Allies had hoped to stop the German invasion of France but the Germans had the advantage of speed and surprise.

On 17 June, France's leader, Marshall Pétain, asked for an honourable ceasefire. The south of France stayed independent and ruled from Vichy. The rest was occupied by the Germans. France looked to the USA for help, but America was still trying to stay out of the war.

Channel Islands occupied

IN JUNE the Channel Islands were taken over by the Germans. (This was the only part of Britain to be occupied during the course of the war.)

Food rationing begins

IN BRITAIN, the new year began with food rationing. People felt this was the fairest way of sharing what was already in short supply. Butter, sugar, ham, bacon and fats were the first to have restrictions. Meat and tea had been added by the summer.

Ration books had coupons that could be exchanged for various foods. The amounts allowed varied somewhat during the war, according to what was available.

Italy comes into the war

IN JUNE, Italy's leader, Mussolini, brought his country into the war – fighting on the German side. In September, a pact was made between Germany, Italy and Japan (the 'New Order').

A small part of the British army was posted in Egypt and Sudan. This was to guard against the threat of invasion from Italian armies. Italy had conquered Ethiopia in 1936 and had forces in Africa far outnumbering the British.

People told: 'don't waste'

'PIGGY BINS' were set up on British street corners. People were required to put all food wastes in these, and the contents were fed to pigs. By July, everyone had to collect salvage. Waste paper and scrap metal, in particular, were needed. Wrought-iron railings were taken down from around many town squares. The metal was used for war weapons. Wasteland was used to grow vegetables and to keep hens, pigs and rabbits. 'Dig for Victory' was one famous slogan.

Churchill becomes PM

MPS IN THE BRITISH HOUSE OF COMMONS called for a debate on 7 May. They were unhappy with how Prime Minister Chamberlain was handling the war. As one MP said that day: 'We must get a government of men of fighting spirit. We are fighting for our lives. We cannot be led as we are.'

The Conservative government's majority fell from over 200 to 80 that day. This signalled the end for Chamberlain. 'Go, go, go! shouted MPs to the Cabinet ministers and to the Prime Minister in particular. Chamberlain was white-faced and strained as he rose and walked slowly out.

Winston Churchill took over as Prime Minister on 10 May. He headed an all-party national government to meet the emergency of war. Churchill offered a strong leadership. He said on taking office: 'You ask what is our aim? I can answer in one word. It is victory.'

Home Guard launched

'NOW IS YOUR OPPORTUNITY' urged Britain's War Minister in a May radio broadcast. Within minutes, local police stations were being swamped. The new civilian groups were called Local Defence Volunteers. These men were to help if the Germans did invade Britain, as was feared at the time.

In July, Churchill renamed the force the 'Home Guard'. Untrained, with makeshift equipment, the volunteers were often men too old (or too young) to be in the services. They were often ridiculed but, in fact, did many useful jobs until the force was disbanded in 1944. The Home Guard took over tasks such as manning anti-aircraft guns and bomb disposal, which freed regular soldiers for the fighting overseas.

Signposts taken down

IN MAY, Britain's Minister of Transport announced that signposts helpful to an invading enemy were to be removed. All along main roads and country lanes signposts were taken down. The aim was to confuse the enemy, if they arrived. Meanwhile, many British people were getting hopelessly lost!

Firewatching compulsory

THE DUTY OF WATCHING for fires started by incendiary bombs became compulsory in Britain. People took their turns on rooftops and put out small fires as they could.

February 1940. Nurses weighed out butter rations once a week. Four ounces were allowed per person.

Helping wartime culture

'WHAT SORT OF MADNESS is this?' asked one British newspaper. The news was that in April the British government voted £50,000 to help wartime culture. CEMA – the Council for the Encouragement of Music and the Arts – went on to support all sorts of cultural activities.

CEMA had 100 artists on 'special assignment'. Many were attached to military units to draw and paint what they saw. Another 200 artists recorded wartime life and sold their pictures to the committee. John Piper was one artist who went round the bombsites. Henry Moore was another war artist. He drew haunting pictures of people sleeping in the Underground during the Blitz. These became a famous reminder of life during the war.

Shelterers in the Tube by war artist Henry Moore. 'I hadn't wanted to be a war artist. . . . One night we came back by tube. I became fascinated by the kind of family life people were living. It reminded me of a slave ship.'

Cinema and theatre boom

PEOPLE IN BRITAIN went to see films and plays as much as they could. Money spent on such entertainment doubled during the war years. Places did close at times, but most carried on. When the Blitz first began, attendance did fall, but it soon recovered. Some cinemas even offered shelter for the night. Many cinemas were destroyed in air raids.

Radio popular

BRITISH TELEVISION had begun in the late 1930s but was shut down during wartime. Radio remained a great favourite for entertainment as well as for news. One popular radio comedy show was 'ITMA' ('It's That Man Again'), starring Tommy Handley. Characters included Mrs Mopp, whose phrase 'Can I do you now, sir?' became a catchphrase of the nation.

Sport much reduced

SPORT WAS PLAYED much less during the war years. Professional and amateur players were either away in the forces or spending hours on war work. Another reason was that sports grounds were needed for other purposes. In the UK, some sports land was used for Home Guard drilling, for growing food, for air raid shelters, or for prisoner-of-war camps.

In 1940 the fear was that the Germans might invade Britain. Golfers were asked to help dig up golf courses where enemy troop planes might try to land. Machine-gun posts were built on some courses.

The crowds coming to watch what sport did take place were less than a quarter of their pre-war size. Sometimes games had to be stopped because of raids by enemy bombers.

A few popular films of 1940:
* *The Great Dictator* starring Charlie Chaplin
* *Fantasia* by Walt Disney
* *Rebecca* by Alfred Hitchcock

A famous novel:
* *For Whom the Bell Tolls* by Ernest Hemingway

Some hit songs:
* 'When or Where'
* 'A Nightingale Sang in Berkeley Square'
* 'In the Mood'
* 'The Lady is a Tramp'

RADAR was used widely in the war. The photo shows a 'skiatron' in 1945, used for tactical plotting to intercept enemy aircraft. It gave a large picture which would be viewed in a well-lit room. A cathode-ray tube gave a dark trace and projected the image by epidiascope methods.

Radar

'RADAR (Radio Detection and Ranging) had been developed in the 1930s to detect and locate far-away objects by the reflection of radio waves. One of its main uses was to give warning of an air attack before enemy planes could be seen or heard. By 1940, the Air Ministry in Britain had a chain of early-warning radar stations along the south and east coasts. These played a large part in winning the Battle of Britain.

Apart from its use in wartime, RADAR became essential for safe navigation of ships, aircraft and even rockets.

Some 'firsts' in 1940

* The tape recorder was sold for the first time in Germany. (The principle for this invention had been discovered long before, in 1898.)
* *Plutonium*, the first artificial element, was made.
* The electron microscope appeared, making new scientific studies possible. This uses an electron beam instead of light, and electro-magnetic forces instead of glass lenses.
* The first car with automatic transmission became available (the Oldsmobile, in the USA).
* The first commercial synthetic tyres were exhibited.
* A continuous coal-digging machine came into use, revolutionizing coal mining.
* A freeze-drying process for preserving food was discovered.
* The first Jeep was designed. (The word came from 'GP', General Purpose field vehicle.)
* Nylon had been patented in 1937, and toothbrush bristles were the first product made. Nylon yarn was produced commercially for the first time in 1939 and the first nylon stockings went on sale in 1940, in the USA. No longer did women have to depend on expensive silk stockings. Artificial silk stockings, made from wood pulp, did not last well when washed regularly, and the alternative cotton lisle ones were thick and unflattering.

Complete MARKETS   **THE CHICAGO DAILY NEWS**   **Sports Final**

66TH YEAR—288.   MONDAY, DECEMBER 8, 1941—THIRTY-FOUR PAGES.   Telephone DEArborn 1111   ★   THREE CENTS

JAP PLANES RAID MANILA!
CONGRESS DECLARES WAR

★   ★   ★   ★   ★   ★

1,500 Die in Hawaii; Coast on Alert

Surprise attack

RADIO BROADCASTS were interrupted at 2.30 pm on 7 December 1941. The amazing news was that much of the American Pacific Fleet, with aircraft, had been destroyed at Pearl Harbour, Hawaii. The Japanese had launched a successful surprise attack. US President Roosevelt was furious that American aircraft were not even in the air defending. 'On the *ground*!' he roared.

Four American battleships were sunk and four more severely damaged. Three destroyers and four smaller vessels were sunk as well. About 188 American planes were lost with another 63 damaged. Over 3400 Americans were killed or wounded. Although the losses were heavy the attack did miss three important aircraft carriers, oil tankers and some other major targets.

Eye-witness account

ONE AMERICAN SAILOR who was in the harbour that Sunday described the attack:

. . . I cannot tell you how many ships were lying in Pearl Harbour that peaceful Sunday morning. That is a naval secret. But you know that Pearl Harbour is the United States' largest naval base – battleships were there, destroyers lay near them, mine-layers, cruisers and all types of ships.

From somewhere a wave of torpedo planes eased down towards the ships and released their torpedos, glittering like fish in the sun, plunging with a loud splash into the sea. Each plane had its object carefully selected in advance for the approaching planes separated and each went to a definite attack.

A massive battleship rocked as if hit by a mighty fist. Almost simultaneously jets of oil spouted all over the ship. In two minutes the deck of the ship was covered with flames. Flames leapt as high as the crow's nest on which a lone sailor stood. Gropingly he leaped into the oil-covered, flaming water below, just missing the deck. When he clambered upon the beach, all the hair had been singed from his head.

At eleven o'clock Dr Pinkerton made a short appeal over the local radio. 'A call for volunteer blood donors! Report immediately to Queens Hospital.' Some people stood in line for seven hours to give their blood. . .
Blake Clark, *Pearl Harbour: An Eyewitness Account*, Bodley Head, 1940

Japan followed its Pearl Harbour attack with other conquests in the Pacific. Although the first months saw a series of Japanese victories the tide later turned in favour of the Allies.

Pearl Harbour

The USS California *sunk in Pearl Harbour after it was bombed by the Japanese.*

America finally at war

AMERICA HAD WANTED to stay out of the war. She was trying to keep to her policy of isolation. With great oceans on either side, America believed she could stay apart from the rest of the world. She had been drawn reluctantly into the First World War, but in the 1930s had passed 'Neutrality Acts'. The 1935 Act gave the President power to forbid American ships from carrying American arms to countries at war.

When the Second World War broke out America agreed to supply arms to her allies. 'We must be the arsenal of democracy' said Roosevelt in a 1940 radio speech. The United States was giving increasing support to Britain. A 'Lend-Lease' agreement was made in March 1941. This let Britain have armaments immediately, with payment delayed.

After the attack on Pearl Harbour, however, America could no longer afford to remain on the sidelines. President Roosevelt asked Congress to declare war and it did this with an overwhelming vote on 8 December.

Relations between America and Japan had been becoming worse for years. By the 1920s America had colonies in the Philippines, Guam and other Pacific islands. She found herself in conflict with Japan's ideas for expansion. By 1940, Japan's empire included Korea, Formosa (later Taiwan), Manchuria and large parts of China. Japan's imperial ambitions were similar to Hitler's plans for conquest in Europe. Japan had joined with Germany and Italy to form the Axis powers. By the end of 1941 the United States was a full member of the opposing 'Grand Alliance'. The other two leading powers were Britain and the Soviet Union.

Churchill was very pleased when America finally joined Britain in the war against the Axis powers. He later wrote:

To have the United States at our side was to me the greatest joy. . . Now at this very moment I knew the United States was in the war, up to the neck and in to death. So we had won after all! . . . Hitler's fate was sealed. Mussolini's fate was sealed. As for the Japanese, they would be ground to powder. . . . No doubt it would take a long time. . . . But there was no more doubt about the end. . . . Being saturated and satiated with emotion and sensation, I went to bed and slept the sleep of the saved and thankful.
W.S. Churchill, *The Grand Alliance*

World News

Atlantic Charter

AMERICAN PRESIDENT ROOSEVELT and British Prime Minister Churchill met onboard ship off the coast of Newfoundland in August 1941. They produced a declaration of ideals which was supported by China, the Soviet Union and 22 other nations.

The Charter included a number of 'principles' which the President and Prime Minister 'deemed it right to make known'. These included 'they desire to see no territorial changes that do not accord with the freely expressed wishes of all the peoples concerned' and 'they hope to see established a peace which will afford to all nations the means of dwelling in safety within their own boundaries.'

Clothes rationing begins

CLOTHES RATIONING BEGAN in Britain in June 1941. Most people welcomed this as the fairest way of sharing what goods were available. Customers could still choose where to shop, and were not registered with one particular store. Some groups, such as older children, had extra coupons.

Wartime rationing and shortages encouraged people to buy clothes of the best quality they could afford, so that they would last. Children's garments, in particular, were in short supply during the war and for a few years after. Adult clothing was somewhat less of a problem, as so many adults went into the forces.

'Utility' clothing was introduced in 1941. Garments were made of specified cloths and prices were closely controlled. All sorts of regulations followed, cutting out much of the unnecessary styling and trimming on garments.

'Make-do-and-mend' was the rule. By 1943 the amount of clothing available for British citizens was about half of what it had been before the war. Spending on clothing fell by over one-third between 1938 and 1944. Mothers were encouraged to cut up and re-use every bit of old garments to clothe their families.

Channel Islands occupied

GERMANY OCCUPIED THE CHANNEL ISLANDS from the middle of 1940. A dispatch was smuggled out in 1941 describing something of conditions for local people:

. . . The British are living on a small basic ration. The island produces fine vegetables and dairy products. This is taken away from the inhabitants. Only 2 oz of butter a week is allowed. One ounce of tea and 2 oz of sugar is the ration. There are no candles, soap, paraffin or salt. Clothes are becoming patched and scarce. The people are wearing wooden clogs because leather has disappeared. There is no thread. This has made it impossible to alter or darn clothes. The Germans have set the men to work making roads. The only entertainment is a cinema show twice a week. The films are German.

Lend-Lease Aid

AMERICA'S NEW LEND-LEASE ACT on 11 March 1941 provided all-out aid to Britain and other countries at war with the Axis powers. This aid continued until June of 1945 and totalled $42,000,000,000. About 42% of American Lend-Lease Aid went to Britain. Nearly half was spent on munitions such as bombers and tanks. Another 24% went on food, 15% on industrial products and 11% on petroleum.

In 1944, American President Roosevelt explained in a speech to Congress that all this contribution by America was not really 'aid':

. . . They include neither gifts, loans or transfer of money. They are . . . a system of mutual war supply . . . to make possible the effective combined operations by which we are fighting and winning the war.

A shopper brings her ration book as clothes rationing starts in the UK.

Germans invade Greece and Yugoslavia

GERMAN TROOPS INVADED Greece and Yugoslavia in April 1941. The Yugoslav government surrendered on 17 April, with the Greeks signing an armistice a few days later.

The capture of Crete was the most striking air operation of the war. On the morning of 20 May about 3000 German parachute troops landed on the island. At the time, Crete was being held by British, Australian and new Zealand troops, along with Greek divisions.

By the first night, the number of Germans on Crete had more than doubled. More parachute troops followed, along with troop-carriers. A total of 22,000 Germans were landed by air. On 26 May the British Commander reported 'Our position here is hopeless'. By 31 May British forces had been evacuated.

German parachutists landed in Crete in a spectacular invasion. Many died in the fall when their parachutes didn't open.

Bismarck sinks

THE GERMAN BATTLESHIP *Bismarck* was sunk by the British navy in the North Atlantic on 27 May 1941. It was a new battleship and managed to survive at least eight torpedo hits and many more hits by shells. This was a key loss in the Battle of the Atlantic, which continued for most of the six years of war.

Vitamin Welfare Scheme starts

A VITAMIN WELFARE SCHEME for British children started in late 1941. There was concern that food rationing might result in children becoming malnourished. Blackcurrant juice (rich in vitamin C) and cod-liver oil (rich in vitamins A and D) were at first issued free for children under two. The juice later became orange, and a small charge was made.

Despite food rationing, people had in some ways healthier diets during wartime, because sugar and sweets in particular were in such short supply.

Germans invade Soviet Union

ON THE MORNING OF 22 JUNE 1941, BBC Radio reported: 'Hitler has announced that his armies are marching against Russia.' Over three million German soldiers poured into the USSR in what was called 'Operation Barbarosa'. The Russians were surprised and suffered heavy losses. The Germans cut off Leningrad and many Russians died of starvation. (More Russians died in the siege of Leningrad than the total war dead of America and Britain combined.)

By early December the German forces were not far from Moscow. But Hitler's men were exhausted and very cold. They did not have clothing for the sub-zero Russian temperatures. Hitler had expected to accomplish his aims before winter began. On 6 December Russian forces counter-attacked and forced the Germans back.

The early months of fighting cost heavy losses on both sides. The Russian army lost over four million soldiers, 15,000 armoured vehicles and 9000 aircraft. Over a million German soldiers were casualties.

Sport and the Arts

Leningrad Symphony

THE RUSSIAN COMPOSER Dmitri Shostakovich wrote his famous symphony, the Leningrad Symphony, in 1941, while the city was under siege by the Germans.

ENSA entertains

ENTERTAINMENTS NATIONAL SERVICE ASSOCIATION (ENSA) was formed in Britain at the start of the war to entertain the troops. It grew into something much wider. Over a thousand factories had at least one ENSA concert in the canteen each week. About 80% of people in the British entertainment industry were ENSA employees. A number of stars began their careers in ENSA (e.g. Tony Hancock, Gracie Fields, George Formby and Vera Lynn).

Comedian Tommy Trinder said ENSA stood for 'Every Night Something Awful'. Much of the entertainment was less than polished, but it *was* wartime. Over the six years two and a half million performances were given, some very close to the dangers of the front line.

Watch on the Rhine performed

AMERICAN PLAYWRIGHT Lillian Hellman wrote *Watch on the Rhine* to alert Americans to the evils of fascism. It was first performed in April of 1941, eight months before the United States entered the Second World War. The drama is set in 1940 in the Washington home of a wealthy widow. Her daughter is married to a German who is part of the anti-Nazi underground. He is blackmailed and the widow comes to realize the full impact of the Nazi threat.

Big band era

'SWING' MUSIC had begun in the mid-1930s, when Benny Goodman formed a band in Los Angeles. Other American band leaders such as Artie Shaw, Tommy Dorsey and Charlie Barnet followed the style. By the early 1940s swing music and big bands were popular in Britain as well. People danced to such songs as 'In the Mood', 'Tuxedo Junction' and 'American Patrol', made popular by band leader Glenn Miller. A few hits songs of 1941 were 'Yours', 'I,Yi,Yi,Yi,Yi (I Like You Very Much)', 'Kiss the Boys Goodbye', 'You Started Something' and 'You Stepped Out of a Dream'.

The Last Tycoon published

AMERICAN NOVELIST F. Scott Fitzerald spent the last years of his life working as a motion picture writer in Hollywood. His novel *The Last Tycoon* is about a studio man and the industry. Fitzgerald died of a heart attack and never finished the book but it was edited and first published in 1941.

Benny Goodman and his band, one of a number of famous bands in the 1940s.

Citizen Kane released

ORSEN WELLES wrote, directed and produced the film *Citizen Kane* in 1941. It is about an American newspaper tycoon whose public-spirited image does not fit with the private views of him and his activities. The parallels with the real-life tycoon Randolf Hearst created a scandal. Regarded as one of the best films ever made, *Citizen Kane* made new use of sound and also wide-angle and deep-focus lenses.

A sentimental song published in 1941 was 'White Cliffs of Dover', which became a favourite throughout the war:

There'll be blue-birds over
The White Cliffs of Dover
Tomorrow, just you wait and see.
There'll be love and laughter
And peace ever after
Tomorrow, when the world is free.

Jet aeroplane

THE FIRST BRITISH jet-propelled aeroplane flew in 1941. Sir Frank Whittle, the inventor, had first thought of the idea in 1929. By the end of the Second World War a British jet fighter aircraft was being produced. There was a rapid increase in the use of jet engines after the war, and by the early 1970s most aircraft were jet powered.

In Whittle's engines, air was drawn in, compressed and mixed with kerosene. The mixture was ignited and this heat caused the gases to expand. Thrust was created by the ejection of a powerful jet of gas.

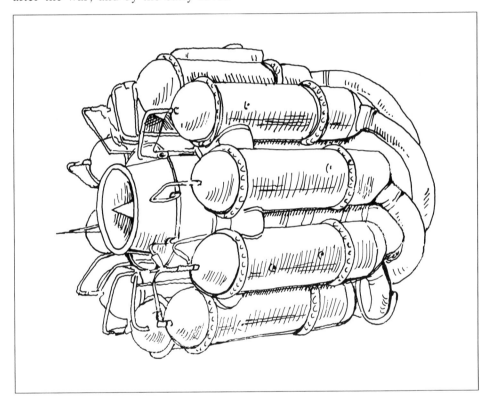

The Whittle W1 Turbojet of 1941.

Aerosol patented

An 'AEROSOL' is a pressurized container with a built-in spray mechanism. The invention has allowed for convenient packaging of everything from deodorants and insecticides to paints and perfumes. The canister contains a fluid under pressure. The pressure is maintained by gas in the upper part of the aerosol. When a valve button is pressed, the fluid is let out in a spray or mist.

While a novelty in the 1940s, aerosols have since been criticized for having some harmful effects on the environment.

Chipboard

PARTICLE BOARD (chipboard) was first manufactured in 1941, in Germany. The shortage of raw materials encouraged Germany and other countries to develop new processes. To make chipboard, wood from thinnings and wastes from industrial timber processing are cut into small chips. These are passed through a grading machine and then dried. The chips are spread out on linked steel plates and then go through cold and hot presses. This consolidates the chips into a firm board.

OSRD set up

THE AMERICAN OFFICE OF SCIENTIFIC RESEARCH AND DEVELOPMENT (OSRD) was set up in 1941 to direct a whole range of war-related research. OSRD worked with scientists in Britain and Canada on problems in a wide number of fields – from medicine and engineering to agriculture and metallurgy.

OSRD successes included more powerful explosives, new types of mines and better aeroplane engines. The results also had implications well beyond the military. Large-scale production of penicillin became possible and the new pesticide DDT was developed. (DDT not only helped control typhus and malaria during wartime, it also contributed to the increase of world food production after the war.) The most significant work of OSRD was the Manhattan Project, which resulted in the atomic bomb.

Some other 'firsts' in 1941
* The first commercial television network (USA).
* The combination peanut-harvester and sheller (USA).
* Terylene, a synthetic polyester fibre (USA).

Towards Stalingrad

AFTER THE SIEGE OF LENINGRAD and the bitter fighting in the winter of 1941-2, Hitler realized he did not have the forces for another general assault. He decided to focus on the southern front for a drive towards the Caucasus, a region of the USSR between the Black and Caspian Seas. This area has over 90% of Russia's oil reserves. Hitler thought that cutting off oil supplies would bring down the Soviets:

The aim is to destroy what armies the Russians have left. Also we must stop the Russians from building up new armies by breaking their economy. All possible forces will be put in the southern area.

One step in this drive towards the Caucasus was the capture of Stalingrad, an important centre of communications on the Volga River. Hitler became obsessed with the idea. The city was a great industrial centre with about half a million inhabitants. For about a month, Stalingrad made preparations for the German attack. The Russian leader, Stalin, sent in a military commander to organize the defence of the city. Women, children and old men were sent to safer areas, and the city's approaches were fortified.

The battle begins

THE ONSLAUGHT AGAINST STALINGRAD began with an air raid on 23 August. Much of the central city was reduced to rubble. The next day, German artillery shelled Soviet positions on the northern edge of the city. Then more troops attacked from the south and the German Sixth Army began closing in. Soviet troops were determined to defend the city. The Germans found themselves in a street-to-street struggle. Casualties on both sides were high. A German soldier reported:

It was a terrible battle – above and below ground, in the ruins, the cellars and the sewers of the great city. Tanks crunched through the ruins, firing at point-blank range. What was worse was that night after night the Russians brought in more men and supplies from the eastern bank of the River Volga.

By 23 November Hitler's Sixth Army was encircled within Stalingrad. On 10 January 1943 the Red Army broke into the city. The German forces were weakened by the months of fighting but they still defended themselves. General Guderin, a German tank commander, wrote in his diary:

The icy cold, the lack of shelter, the shortage of clothing, the heavy losses of men and equipment, the wretched state of our fuel supplies – all this makes the duties of a commander a misery, and the longer it goes on the more I am crushed by the enormous responsibility I have to bear.

Nazi soldiers enter a captured factory in Stalingrad. Russians destroyed the factory rather than let it fall into enemy hands.

in Stalingrad

Turning point in war

THE EVENTS IN STALINGRAD were a turning point of the war. It was Germany's first major defeat. Hitler's big mistake in attacking Russia was that he was fighting wars on two fronts. However, he felt a special need to conquer the Soviet Union.

Communism, and its ideas of equality, represented everything he hated. He saw it as his mission to overrun the Slavic *Untermenschen* ('subhumans') in the East, so his own superior Aryan master race would have more space and resources.

It was the end of January before German resistance collapsed. The Russians took 91,000 prisoners – all that was left of the original 285,000 men of the German Sixth Army. A lieutenant of the XXIV Panzer Division described the scene:

And imagine Stalingrad; eighty days and eighty nights of hand-to-hand struggles. The street is no longer measured by metres but by corpses. . .

On 1 February 1943, the *Daily Mail* reported:

STALINGRAD ARMY WIPED OUT
16 Axis Generals captured
Field-Marshall Paulis, Commander-in-Chief of the German Sixth Army and Fourth Tank Army at Stalingrad, was captured by the Russians yesterday a few hours after he had been promoted to the highest rank by special proclamation from Hitler's headquarters.

He was seized with his staff when Soviet troops stormed the headquarters in the heart of the city and completed the greatest disaster that has befallen Germany in the war. . .

Casualties of German soldiers were especially high on the Russian front. Hitler: 'I have the right to demand of each soldier that he should give up his life if need be.'

Germans pushed back

SOVIET WAR PRODUCTION was at full speed by the spring of 1942. America and British lend-lease aid was helping to supply over 10% of Russia's war needs. Russian generals were experienced by then with German strategy and tactics. As Russia's ability to resist grew, so Germany was being weakened. German air power, weaponry and manpower were being depleted. But German troops in Russia were still not beaten, however, as the events of Summer 1943 would show.

"I AM RESPONSIBLE FOR THE PRESENT OF THE GERMAN PEOPLE . . . AND THEIR FUTURE"—HITLER

Battle of El Alamein

WAR HAD STARTED IN THE MIDDLE EAST in September 1940. An Italian army from Libya invaded Egypt so it could attack British forces there. British troops counter-attacked and drove them back into Libya. The Italians were reinforced in March 1941 by a German army commanded by General Rommel. He forced the British to retreat into Egypt.

The British army started a new offensive in November 1941. General Rommel pushed his German troops into Egyptian territory until they were stopped at El Alamein. At the famous Battle of El Alamein, General Montgomery led a force of British, Australian, New Zealand and Indian soldiers and finally drove the Germans and Italians from North Africa. On 5 November 1942 the Daily Mirror jubilantly reported:

ROMMEL ROUTED
Huns fleeing in disorder
9000 men captured
260 tanks destroyed
600 planes knocked out
Rommel's desert army, blitzed as no German army has ever been blitzed before, is in full retreat with the Eighth Army in close pursuit of his 'disordered' columns.

The dramatic story of General Montgomery's smashing victory was told in the following special joint communiqué from British Headquarters in Cairo last night:

North African patrols in the Western Desert gathered information about enemy activities.

"The Axis forces in the Western Desert, after twelve days and nights of ceaseless attacks by our land and air forces, are now in full retreat. Their disordered columns are being relentlessly attacked by our land forces and by the Allied Air Force by day and night. . . ."

Allies land in French North Africa

ALLIED TROOPS LANDED in French North Africa on 8 November 1942. Churchill had put forward the idea of a 'North-West Africa Project' as a way of 'closing and tightening the ring around Germany'. 'Operation Torch', as it was called, was led by General Dwight D. Eisenhower. Eisenhower played a central role in the war, leading the

Allied forces. Just after the war he commented:

The hard task of a commander is to send men into battle knowing some of them – often many – must be killed or wounded in order that necessary missions may be achieved. It is a soul-killing task. . . .

Utility furniture starts

SIMPLE, 'UTILITY' FURNITURE was first produced in Britain in 1942. By 1943 this limited range was all that was being made. Wartime pressure on resources meant that there was only enough for the most urgent needs. Licences to buy the furniture were given first to people who had been bombed out or were setting up home for the first time. Many articles came under the utility scheme, including home electrical appliances and carpets.

Households became increasingly shabby, as replacement of household items was so difficult. In Britain, spending on household goods fell by nearly two-thirds between 1938 and 1944.

Black equality

IN JULY 1942 the American movie industry publicly stated that American 'Negroes' would be shown as a full part of American life. They would no longer be restricted to comic and menial parts. It took decades for this intention to become reality, but it was part of moves in the 1940s towards black equality. Discrimination in employment, housing and schooling was still widespread but efforts were beginning.

In the 1940s segregation was still strong in the American south, and literacy tests kept many Blacks from voting. Only about 3% of American Blacks were registered voters.

Marines land on Guadalcanal

AMERICAN MARINES LANDED ON GUADALCANAL in the Japanese-occupied Solomon Islands in August 1942. By the following January there were over 50,000 well-supplied American troops. The Japanese, meanwhile, were much weakened by hunger and malaria. In February 1943 the Japanese troops withdrew. The long struggle for Guadalcanal had been a serious defeat for Japan.

Battle of Coral Sea

JAPANESE EXPANSION in the south-west Pacific was halted by the May 1942 Battle of the Coral Sea. This was the first battle in history to be fought by fleets that never actually saw each other. Long-range weapons were used.

Pacific war

JAPANESE SUCCESSES IN THE PACIFIC in 1942 included the invasion of the Dutch East Indies (January), and the seizure of Singapore (February) and Burma (March). In June, the Japanese naval force attacked Midway Island in the central Pacific, but was stopped by American ships and planes.

Laval heads Vichy regime

ON 11 NOVEMBER 1942 THE GERMANS took over the rest of unoccupied France. Pierre Laval was made head of their puppet Vichy regime.

Laval was a French lawyer who became prime minister of France in the 1930s. He thought a German victory in the war was inevitable and decided full collaboration was the best course to take. In 1942 he agreed to provide French workers for German industry and even said he *wanted* Germany to win the war.

In 1945, after the war, Pierre Laval was tried for treason and executed.

Japanese interned

BY EARLY 1942 there was much resentment against Japanese-Americans living in America. About 110,000 of these civilians were rounded up into 'relocation camps', with barracks on government land. These were surrounded by barbed wire and guards. It was the end of 1944 before the Japanese men, women and children were released.

Beveridge Report

THE BEVERIDGE REPORT came out in December 1942, and 90% of the population favoured the ideas it put forward. The plan was for a single overall scheme of social insurance, to include a new National Health Service and family allowances for children. After the war, the ideas of the Beveridge Report became the basis for the new 'welfare state'.

Utility furniture was displayed at the Building Centre in London.

L'Etranger published

THE FRENCH EXISENTIALIST WRITER Albert Camus published a novel called *L'Étranger* ("The Outsider") in 1942. This is the story of a man who kills pointlessly, and illustrates Camus' belief that human existence is absurd. The man's attitude remains listless as he is condemned:

. . . a rush of memories went through my mind – memories of a life which was mine no longer and had once provided me with the surest, humblest pleasures: warm smells of summer, my favourite streets, the sky at evening . . . the futility of what was happening seemed to take me by the throat. . . .

Blithe Spirit published

NOËL COWARD'S PLAY *Blithe Spirit* was first published in 1942 after performances in London the previous year. It was very popular and became one of his most successful plays. Coward later described how the play came to be written:

Joyce Carey [a fellow writer] and I caught a moving train from Paddington, bound for Port Meirion in North Wales. For some time the idea for a light comedy had been rattling at the door of my mind and I thought that the time had come to let it in and show it a little courtesy. . . . We arrived on a golden evening, sighed with pleasure at the mountains and the sea in the late sunlight and settled ourselves into a pink guest-house. The next morning we sat on the beach with our backs against the seawall and discussed my idea exclusively for several hours. . . . By lunchtime the title had emerged together with the names of the characters and a rough – very rough – outline of the plot. At seven-thirty the next morning I sat, with the usual nervous palpitations, at my typewriter. . . . There was a pile of virgin paper on my left and a box of carbons on my right. The table wobbled and I had put a wedge under one of its legs. . . . I fixed the paper into the machine and started: 'Blithe Spirit: A Light Comedy in Three Acts'.

In 1958 Coward said of the play:

I shall be ever grateful for the almost psychic gift that enabled me to write 'Blithe Spirit' in five days during one of the darkest years of the war.

Calder's 'horizontal spines'

AMERICAN SCULPTOR ALEXANDER CALDER trained as an engineer and wanted an art that reflected mathematical ideas. He had the notion that the universe is in constant motion but held together by balancing forces. The idea of balance inspired his mobiles. Various shapes and colours were made to sway in space.

Alexander Calder's 'Standing Mobile' was made in 1942 from painted metal.

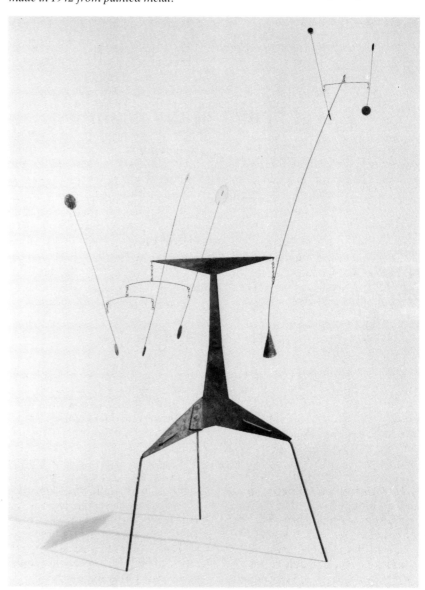

The war prompted many advances in aircraft. A single-seater naval aircraft, the Grumman F4F-4 Wildcat fighter, was a mainstay of the American navy in 1942. The planes could operate from small escort carriers.

The helicopter

THE FIRST HELICOPTER in manufactured production appeared in 1942. The idea for a machine which rose vertically by the use of a horizontal propeller had originally been developed as a toy. A string was pulled to set the helicopter soaring, but no steering was possible.

In the early 1900s several inventors had managed to make *real* machines that rose vertically, but steering was still a problem. It was not until 1924 that a helicopter which could be directed once in the air was designed. In 1939 Igor Sikorsky built a prototype VS-300, which was the basis of the modern machine.

Atomic reactor built

AN ALL-OUT EFFORT in atomic research began in 1941. Nuclear physicists knew that two uranium derivatives – U-235 and plutonium – could be used to undergo rapid fission. This is when a neutron penetrates a nucleus of uranium – 235. The nucleus splits and gives off even more neutrons, as well as energy. Occasionally, fission may happen spontaneously. If neutrons from the fission of one nucleus go on to split other nuclei, a chain reaction may result. Scientists faced the problem of how to control a chain reaction, how to produce enough of the fissionable material and how to translate the theories into a workable bomb.

Enrico Fermi solved the first problem on 2 December 1942. In a laboratory under the University of Chicago athletic stadium he directed the first controlled chain reaction. It showed that nuclear fission could be started, contained and then stopped. The first nuclear reactor was a 19-ft (6m) high, 24½-ft (8m) square mixture of uranium and graphite bricks.

The secret 'Manhattan Project' went on to develop a workable bomb, first used over Hiroshima in 1945.

Rockets launched

THE SPACE AGE REALLY BEGAN in 1942, with the launch of the German V-2 rocket. Wernher von Braun's V-2 was a weapon which flew at several times the speed of sound, giving no warning as it approached. It carried a one-tonne warhead of the highly explosive Amatol. The V-2's engine was the predecessor of all of today's long-range rocket engines.

A rocket engine is different from a jet engine in that it doesn't draw oxygen from the air to burn fuel. Rocket engines use their own oxygen, carried within the rocket casings. It is because of this that rocket engines can work outside the earth's atmosphere.

Besides working on the V-2, German scientists developed a variety of liquid – and solid – propellant rocket vehicles for military use. Other nations (the US, Britain, the Soviet Union and Japan) developed solid-propellant rockets during the war. But the Germans were the only ones to make use of the large, liquid-propellant rocket. The team, headed by Von Braun, surrendered to the American forces and was brought to the US in 1946.

1943 Death camps

Camps killing millions

BY 1943 A TERRIBLE SYSTEM of death camps was in full operation in Europe. Some labour camps had been started in 1933 as places where the German Nazis could send their opponents. By the late 1930s and early 1940s these were being used for Jews and other minorities. There were six camps in Germany in 1939, with about 20,000 prisoners.

During the Second World War the number of camps increased. More were built in Germany and Poland. Conditions were brutal. People were given little food. They were beaten, kept in crude, overcrowded barracks and forced to do hard labour. Some prisoners were used for barbaric medical experiments. People were gassed, burned, shot, hung, tortured and treated with great cruelty.

Dachau was one of the most dreaded of the camps. Many prisoners threw themselves on the electric wire fences rather than face the terrible conditions.

Adolf Hitler's plan was to create a German 'master race'. This involved systematically murdering what he called 'inferior' people. Over five million people were killed or died from disease and starvation in Hitler's concentration camps. Most of the victims were Jews.

'Waiting for death'

PHILIP MECHANICUS WAS A DUTCH JEW who kept a secret diary of life in a Dutch camp in 1943, waiting for deportation to the death camps of eastern Europe. (Mechanicus was shot in Auschwitz camp, Poland, in 1944.)

Sunday, May 30th, 1943
The Jews are living here . . . without possessions. . . . A suit and some underclothes to cover their miserable limbs in the daytime and a blanket at night, a pair of shoes, a cap, a knife, fork and spoon and a mug are their only belongings. . .
Tuesday, June 1st
The transports [trucks used for transport] are as loathsome as ever. . . . The deportees no longer lie on straw but on the bare floor. . . . Quiet men with tense faces and women bursting into frequent sobs. . .
Friday, November 5th
Icy cold this morning. . . . Bitterly cold in the huts. Two base-burning stoves in the hut, one of which is a miserable little thing which burns badly and gives off little heat. . .
Monday, November 8th
I am sleeping three tiers up and each time I have the same problem – how do I get up? There is no ladder or chair available. You have to clamber along the edges of the bedstead. . . . When the man below me coughs, my bed quivers . . . like a leaf in the wind. The bed is the symbol of the camp – we are on a journey, a voyage in a creaking ship on a heaving ocean. . .

in Europe

Survivors tell of horrors

SOME OF THOSE TRANSPORTED to concentration camps did manage to survive. Elie Wiesel was a teenage boy who was sent to the death camp of Auschwitz and later to Buchenwald. After the war he wrote a book about his experiences, dedicated to his mother, father and sister, all of whom had died in the camps.

Elie Wiesel described how Jews in his home in Hungary were first 'restricted' by the Germans:

Jews would not be allowed to leave their houses for three days. . . . Then a Jew no longer had the right to keep in his house any objects of value. Everything had to handed over to the authorities – on pain of death. . . . We were no longer allowed to go into restaurants or to travel on the railway. Then came the ghetto [Jews were forced to live in a small area of streets, with barbed wire fencing them in.]

Jews were then systematically deported to the death camps. They were crammed into railway cattle wagons, with little air, food or water. On arrival at the camps, some were 'selected' for death straightaway. Elie Wiesel described his arrival at Auschwitz:

. . . As the train stopped, we saw that flames were gushing out of a tall chimney into the black sky. . . . There was an abominable odour floating in the sky. . . . In the air that smell of burning flesh. . .

As Elie was marched through the camp he saw flames in a pit:

They were burning something. A lorry drew up at the pit and delivered its load – little children. Babies! . . . I could not believe it. . . . How could it be possible for them to burn people and for the world to keep silent.

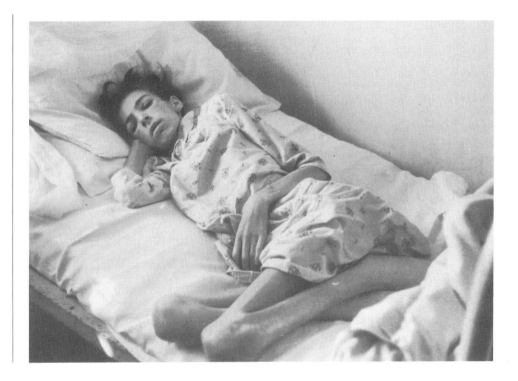

After surviving the harsh conditions of Auschwitz Elie Wiesel was moved to Buchenwald camp. He described the journey. Men, reduced to skin and bone from living on meagre rations of soup and bread, were packed into railway carriages. There was no roof and heavy snow was falling:

We were given no food. We lived on snow. . . . All through those ten days and nights we stayed crouching, one on top of the other, never speaking a word. We were no more than frozen bodies. . . . We waited merely for the next stop so that we could unload our dead. . . . One day when we stopped, a passing German worker took a piece of bread out of his bag and threw it into the wagon. There was a stampede. Dozens of starving men fought each other to the death for a few crumbs. . .
Elie Wiesel, *Night*, Penguin, 1981

A Jewish 13-year-old suffering from starvation, typhus and tuberculosis, after she was rescued from Bergen-Belsen concentration camp. When the British liberated the camp in 1945 they discovered over 40,000 men and women in extreme states of starvation. There were over 13,000 unburied corpses.

Liberation

WHEN THE WAR ENDED Allied troops liberated the concentration camps. The world was shocked as newsreels showed the surviving inmates, many like skeletons and more dead than alive. Mass graves were found with the remains of bodies killed in the genocide.

World News

Perón comes to power

JUAN PERÓN LED A PRO-FASCIST COUP in Argentina in 1943, resulting in the downfall of the Argentinian government. Three years later he was elected president of the country. He began a programme of economic reform and industrialization. Although a dictator, he was very popular with the mass of people. His social welfare programmes brought help to the poorer classes. Eva Perón (Evita), his wife, was active as well. (Perón was exiled in 1955. He returned to Argentina in 1973 to form a government, but died the following year.)

Italy surrenders

ALLIED FORCES HAD LANDED in Morocco, Algeria and Tunisia in November 1942. These soldiers had combined with the British army moving in from Egypt. In May 1943 the German and Italian armies in North Africa surrendered. That summer, Allied forces occupied Sicily and they invaded the Italian mainland in September.

Mussolini's fascist régime was overthrown in the summer of 1943. Britain's Prime Minister, Churchill, made a statement to the House of Commons on 27 July on the downfall of Mussolini:

The House will have heard with satisfaction of the downfall of one of the principal criminals in this desolating war. . . . The keystone of the Fascist arch has crumbled. . .

A new government, under Badoglio, made the surrender and declared war on Germany (13 October). The

On 13th October Marshall Badoglio announced Italy's decision to enter the war on the side of the Allies. (Next to Badoglio is Brigadier General Maxwell Taylor of the American Army.)

following proclamation was read by Marshal Badoglio to the Italian people over the radio:

Italians! There will not be peace in Italy so long as a single German remains on our soil. Shoulder to shoulder we must march forward with our friends of the United States, of Great Britain, of Russia. . . .

Germany sent forces into Italy and there was much hard fighting. It was not until the spring of 1945 that the German soldiers were completely driven out of Italy.

Bevin Boys scheme begins

THE WARTIME SHORTAGE OF MINERS in Britain prompted Ernest Bevin, then Minister of Labour, to direct youths to work in the mines as part of their National Service. From the end of 1943, 10% of boys reaching military service age were chosen by ballot to be 'Bevin Boys'. About 45,000 boys from all social classes eventually found themselves in this unpopular service.

Terror in Poland

THE POLISH GOVERNMENT handed a report to the Allied governments in December 1942 about German atrocities in occupied Poland. Another note followed in January 1943. Throughout 1943 there was terror in Poland as thousands of men, women and children fell victims. In November 1943, the Polish National Council made a statement in London about what had been happening to Jews in particular.

Between September 1939 and July 1942 about 130,000 Warsaw Jews died of starvation and in slave labour camps. . . . Between July and September 1942 the population of the Warsaw Ghetto was reduced from 350,000 to 120,000 by deportation, shootings, and mass slaughter in death camps. The last phase began on September 5, when the German authorities announced that, as from 1 October 1942, the Ghetto would be issued with only 40,000 ration books. . . . German-owned factories in Warsaw informed their Jewish labourers that only one-third of them would henceforth be permitted to work. A few days later the entire Jewish population of Warsaw was assembled and all those not possessing the new labour cards sent to Treblinka [north-east of Warsaw] and other camps for mass execution; the streets were lined with Gestapo men who shot on the spot any people offering the slightest resistance, including any women or children who wept. . .

The Council also described what happened in April 1943 when the remaining Jews in the Warsaw Ghetto fought back:

The Ghetto battle . . . commenced on April 19 after the German authorities had decided on the final 'liquidation' of the Warsaw Ghetto. . . . When S.S. [special Nazi police corps] troops entered the Ghetto on that date they were met by fierce resistance from the entire population who had received from the Polish underground movement some arms to defend themselves. From April 19-28 fierce fighting raged unabashed, the Jews fighting back with rifles, machine-guns and even their bare fists against German regular and S.S. troops, who closed all outlets (even the sewers) and used artillery, tanks and bombers against the Ghetto. After heroic but hopeless resistance . . . the survivors (about 14,000) were deported to Eastern Poland and the Ghetto finally wiped out.

Be careful what you say + where you say it!

CARELESS TALK COSTS LIVES

Wartime posters urged the British to 'Buy War Bonds', not to waste, and to be careful what was said ('Be Like Dad, Keep Mum').

Pacific war

AS THE WAR CONTINUED IN EUROPE, so struggles in the Pacific went on as well. Some key events in 1943 were the evacuation of Japanese forces from Guadalcanal (February) and American General Douglas MacArthur's landing in New Guinea (June). By November, American forces had invaded the Gilbert Islands and crushed resistance by the Japanese.

Operation Citadel

IN THE SUMMER OF 1943 Hitler ordered an offense around Kursk in the USSR. He wanted a victory that would 'shine like a beacon around the world'. The attack was code-named Operation Citadel and began in early July. This ended in Soviet victory, which was yet another blow to Germany's growing losses. Germany was now on the defensive and being pushed back. By the end of 1943, Russia's army outnumbered the Germans by nearly three million men. Russia also had thousands more tanks and heavy guns.

Hamburg is bombed

DR JOSEPH GOEBBELS, a leading German Nazi, wrote in his diary on 29 July 1943:

During the night over 800 English bombers raided Hamburg. A city of a million people has been destroyed. It has given us problems that are impossible to deal with. Food must be found. Shelter must be found. There are 800,000 homeless people wandering up and down the streets, not knowing what to do.

Guggenheim design started

FRANK LLOYD WRIGHT WAS ONE OF AMERICA'S great architects and one of the most important architects this century. His career spanned over 70 years and included various styles. In 1943 he began designing a modern art museum for New York City. The plans were drawn over the years 1943-6, though the museum itself was not built until the late 1950s. Wright's Guggenheim Museum is a circular shape, in concrete. Visitors view works of art by walking along a continuous circular ramp.

Kandinsky painting

A NEW PAINTING BY Vasily Kandinsky attracted attention in 1943. Called 'Circle and Square No. 716', it showed the artist's use of colour and ordered arrangement of spheres and rectangles. Kandinsky was a Russian expressionist who influenced the work of many other artists. (Expression was a revolt against impressionism, a turning away from outer life to what was happening inside the artist.)

Fifth Symphony

RALPH VAUGHAN WILLIAMS WAS AN ENGLISH composer who drew inspiration from folk songs, and sixteenth-century England in particular. His Fifth Symphony was written between the years 1938-43, using themes from his opera 'The Pilgrim's Progress'. He never expected to finish the opera, but did so in 1949.

Casablanca, a famous 1943 film, starred Humphrey Bogart and Ingrid Bergman. Bogart is the owner of Rick's Bar in wartime Casablanca. He discovers that a Resistance worker, whose escape to the US he is aiding, is the husband of his lost love.

'Wave' by Hepworth

BARBARA HEPWORTH WAS AN IMPORTANT English sculptor who produced some of the her most lyrical works between the years 1943 and 1947. She was then working at St Ives in Cornwall. 'Wave' was produced in 1943, out of painted carved wood and string. Hepworth worked abstractly in concrete, bronze, wood and aluminium, but her favourite medium was stone.

'Broadway Boogie-Woogie'

THE UNLIKELY TITLE OF PIET MONDRIAN'S new painting in 1943 was inspired by jazz music at the time. Mondrian was a Dutch abstract painter who helped found the movement known as 'De Stijl' ('The Style'). Its followers tried to apply the principles of geometrical abstract design to painting, sculpture and architecture.

Sartre's 'Existentialism'

THE FRENCH WRITER AND PHILOSOPHER Jean-Paul Sartre published *L'être et le néant* ('Being and Nothingness') in 1943, his first full statement of existentialism. In 1945 the first two parts of the three-volume novel *Les Chemins de la Liberté* ('The Roads to Freedom') were published, also expressing his philosophical ideas.

Sarte's 'existentialism' says that God does not exist, but people are free to give meaning to their lives by what they do. People will be judged by their acts. Existentialist philosophy had much impact on French life and literature after the Second World War.

'Oklahoma!' opens

THE MUSICAL 'OKLAHOMA!' by Rogers and Hammerstein opened in New York in 1943. The romantic story takes place during the settling of the American West and was just what America wanted to take her mind off the war.

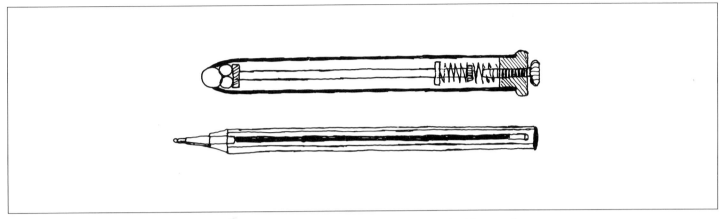

The first-known 'ball-point' (top) patented in 1888, compared with a modern type pen as pioneered in the 1940s.

Ball-point pen

TWO HUNGARIAN BROTHERS, Ladislao and George Biro, patented the modern type of ball-point pen in 1943. Ladislao had been working as a proof-reader for a printer. He was always having to fill his fountain pen and blot the wet ink. He was determined to make a new, clean pen that did not need filling.

It was when the brothers moved to Argentina in 1943 that their invention attracted interest. An English businessman helped set up a factory in England making the new pens for pilots in the RAF. (Fountain pens were not suitable for use in aeroplanes, because pressure changes when flying made the pens likely to leak.) The factory was taken over by a French company, Bic, after the war and sales became more widespread.

The idea of a ball-point pen had been thought of in America as early as 1888. A marker with a ball in its nib was patented, but this was not intended to replace the fountain pen for everyday writing.

Penicillin

THE DISCOVERY OF PENICILLIN dates back to 1928. A Scotsman, Alexander Fleming, noticed that on a dish of gelatine on which he had grown harmful bacteria there was a patch free from bacterial colonies. This was surrounded by mould. He discovered that a substance from the mould, *Penicillium notatum*, prevented the growth of some bacteria.

It was 15 years later, however, before it was possible to produce penicillin on a large scale, using new techniques of deep fermentation. This made it available to doctors and patients. Penicillin became the first, and still is the most effective, antibiotic used in medicine. It has been a great help in the control of disease.

During the war, the 'wonder drug' was used on many cases needing emergency treatment. It saved thousands of soldiers' lives. In 1943 it was being used on men wounded in North Africa and Sicily. For the first time, penicillin was put directly into wounds instead of into the bloodstream.

First artificial kidney

WILHELM J. KOLFF, a Dutch doctor, made the first artificial kidney in 1943. This was the first time a machine replaced a main body organ. The machine took a patient's blood through a water bath with a filter of cellophane wrapped around a wooden frame. Poisons in the bloodstream were diffused through the cellophane, while the blood cells and protein were kept. Short-term treatment could be provided while damaged kidneys were removed. It was not until the 1960s that regular long-term filtering became possible.

Strange happenings

THE IDEA OF ESP (extra-sensory perception) was being explored scientifically in the 1930s and 1940s. In 1941 and 1943 data was published showing that some people could affect events at a distance. This is now known as 'psychokinesis' (or 'PK').

**INVASION GOING WELL:
TANKS ASHORE**

Our invasion is 'proceeding to plan – and what a plan'. This is what a confident Mr Churchill told the House of Commons today in a brief review of the landings in Northern France which began soon after dawn. An immense armada of upward of 4000 ships with several thousand smaller craft have crossed the Channel, sustained by about 11,000 first-time aircraft, disclosed the Premier.

Front page of The Daily Sketch, *6 June 1944*

The longest day

ON 5 JUNE 1944 AMERICAN General Dwight D. Eisenhower studied the weather for the next day. 'O.K., let's go' he said. It was 6 June 1944 (D-Day) when a large force of British, American and Canadian soldiers landed on France's Normandy coast. Before the troops launched the invasion for liberation, each man was handed a copy of an Order of the Day. In that, General Eisenhower told his troops that the eyes of the world were on them and that 'the hopes and prayers of liberty-loving people everywhere much with you. We will accept nothing less than full victory.'

The invasion to liberate Europe had been planned for two years. Much preparation was needed. Around the inlets of the Thames estuary, construction firms poured concrete into **caissons** (watertight cases used in laying foundations under water). The concrete blocks were moved to Sussex, where they were fitted together. On D-Day these were towed across the Channel. These 'Mulberries' supplied 15 miles of piers, causeways and breakwaters. ('Mulberries' was the code name for the huge prefabricated harbours used on D-Day.)

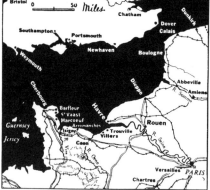

Front page of the Daily Mirror, *7 June 1944.*

The Germans suspected an invasion but thought it would come in the Pas de Calais. The British had used successful tricks to deceive them, such as putting dummy gliders on a Kentish airfield.

Before the landings in Normandy there was a heavy attack by Allied bombers on German batteries along the French coast.

Landing

Personal reminiscences

Mr E.A. Neale:

June 6 1944 was not a very good day weatherwise, being very wet, with galeforce winds . . . not the sort of weather to make a landing on a beach. The invasion had already been delayed and it was now or never, bad weather or not. . . . As we left Southampton we felt the full force of the weather, waves were about thirty to thirty-five feet high and the ship was thrown about like a cork . . . it wasn't long before the troops were feeling the effects. . . .

Troops and supply trucks headed for the front lines on the beaches of Normandy.

Mr Richard Harris:

Trembling, my rifle tightly clenched, I crouched awaiting the dreaded shout of 'Ramps down'. . . . On the order to go, I leapt up, bounded down the ramps, jumped and landed in about four feet of cold sea water. . . . I managed to hold my rifle clear of the water and waded as quickly as I was able to the shallows and the beach. . . . On the beach it was all very confused. Between the crunch of mortar bombs and the whizzing sounds of shells and chunks of metal flying about I remember hearing cries of 'Stretcher bearer' and one plaintive, youthful voice repeatedly calling 'Help me, boys' and then breaking off into shuddering sobs. . . .

Mr V.J. Galliano:

Troops were pouring in: it was a human flood. . . . [At] dusk we . . . moved to cover for the night. . . . Two of us found a convenient trench. . . . Lying on my back at the bottom of the pit, tin hat covering my face, I tried to doze off but there wasn't a chance. Directly our fighters returned to base after dark and Jerry [German] planes came out and at regular intervals throughout the night we were heavily strafed [bombarded]. . . . Shortly after we received another severe drenching from machine-gun and cannon fire delivered at what must have been fairly low level . . . we had to snatch what sleep we could. . . .

Dr Peter Johnson:

Mine casualties by day were very common and some were most frightful to see. My most vivid recollection was being called to see a man . . . lying on a door in the back of a truck. All was covered with a blanket save for his head. He had no face that was not raw and torn. . . . He was conscious and moaning. I put my hand under the blanket and felt for his wrist. To my horror, all I could find was a bloody stump. . . .

Philip Warner (ed.), *The D-Day Landings*, a collection of accounts of personal experiences, William Kimber, 1980

Germans forced to retreat

THERE WAS FIERCE FIGHTING in Normandy and the Germans were forced to retreat. General Montgomery, who was in command of the land forces from Britain, Canada and America, felt confident about D-Day's success:

I don't know when the war is going to end but I don't believe the Germans can go on much longer with this business.

World News

Bombers hit German cities

AMERICAN AIRCRAFT bombed German industrial cities in February 1944, inflicting heavy damage. This was one of the greatest aerial bombardments of the war. Over four times as many bombs were dropped in 1944, as had been in 1943. Berlin was particularly badly hit.

The Warsaw rising

FOR TWO AND A HALF MONTHS in 1944 the Polish people of Warsaw rose courageously against the German occupation. The Poles had ammunition for only seven days of fighting and for the first two days they were doing well. The Germans had been surprised as people took to the streets. Russia gave

Butler Act passed

AN IMPORTANT ACT affecting education in Britain was passed in 1944. The Butler Act made a number of key changes. It said that every child should receive some kind of secondary education. Before the Butler Act, Local Education Authorities were only required by law to provide elementary education for children. Now, a selection test called the 'eleven-plus' was set up to direct every child at age 11 into either grammar school, junior technical school or secondary modern school. Also, for the first time, schools were required to give some religious instruction.

some aid to the Polish rising. However, in the end, the superiority of German firepower won, and the Poles were crushed.

Buzz bombs on Britain

IN JUNE 1944 THE GERMANS started dropping a new type of VI flying bomb on Britain. These were also called 'buzz bombs' or 'doodlebugs'. About 8000 of these bombs caused much damage that summer.

From September onwards V2 rockets were being used. Over a thousand of these fell between September 1944 and March 1945, when the bombing of Britain ended. On 7 September, MP Duncan Sandys, chairman of the 'Flying Bomb Counter-Measures Committee' made a statement to the press:

During the 80 days of the bombardment the enemy has launched over 8000 bombs. Of these some 2300 got through into the London region. Even of the bombs successfully launched, some 25% were inaccurate or erratic. Many dived into the ssea of their own accord. Others strayed as far as Norfolk and Northampton. The remainder were brought down by the combined efforts of guns, fighters and balloons. . . .

Also on 7 September, the government ordered the end of organized evacuation from Greater London and Southern England except for expectant mothers, the infirm, blind persons and invalids (for whom it would continue). In view of heavy damage to property in the London areas (about 870,000 houses still awaited repair) evacuees were urged not to return to the capital yet. The Ministry of Health announced that about 23,000 houses had been totally destroyed or damaged beyond repair by flying-bombs and that the total number of people evacuated at that time was 305,564 (from Greater London and from South East England).

Lionel King was just eight at the time and was living in east London. He kept a diary and later wrote about 'Buzz Bomb Summer' as part of his autobiography:

"It's ridiculous to say these flying bombs have affected people in ANY way."

Thousands of French people cheered as American soldiers moved through liberated Paris in August.

The first came over one afternoon. Our windows and door were open in those fine June days and the drone of the approaching flying bomb was quite unmistakable. It gave us little warning. Ten seconds and the engine cut out directly overhead. There was an oddly resounding explosion about half a mile away . . . soon, so many VIs were coming over the authorities gave up air-raid warnings. They would have been sounding the siren all the time. . . .

When the V2 rockets started, they were even more frightening, because you could not hear them coming:

The fall of a rocket during school hours shattered our concentration. . . . One occasion, just before noon, my attention was distracted by a flicker of light upon the wall just above my eye-level. I glanced at the window and, at that precise moment, a resounding explosion shook the whole school. . . .

Quoted in Michael Moynihan (ed.), *People at War, 1939-1945*, David and Charles, 1974

De Gaulle speaks

THE ALLIED FORCES WERE ADVANCING well through France by July 1944. On 19 August French resistance forces rose in revolt against the Germans. The Germans finally surrendered control of Paris on 25 August, after four years of occupation. By late September all of France, except for areas of Alsace-Lorraine, had been liberated. General de Gaulle spoke in Paris on 25 August and then toured liberated French cities in September/October addressing large crowds. At Lille he said:

Let us not hide the fact, we are a great but impoverished nation. Communications are everywhere cut, canal locks are blown up, the ports are useless, the factories lack coal and primary materials. Nevertheless . . . we shall be in all the battles . . . to the end. . . .

GI Bill of Rights

AMERICA PASSED a GI Bill of Rights in 1944. It offered loans and assistance to ex-servicemen. About half of American college students in 1946 were war veterans. Millions more were able to buy houses on very easy terms.

Plot to kill Hitler fails

On 20 July 1944 there was an attempt to kill Hitler at his Rastenburg headquarters in East Prussia. The bomb missed its target but caused considerable confusion. After the explosion telegrams had been sent from the headquarters to members of the conspiracy saying that Hitler had been killed.

The failed attempt caused much upset and suspicion amongst the German High Command. Generals did not dare to oppose any of Hitler's plans, however foolhardy. Hitler himself became more doubting and would take suggestions only from generals he particularly trusted.

Battle of the Bulge

Hitler mustered his forces during autumn 1944 for a decisive assault. In a sudden offensive at dawn on 16 December, the Germans struck at Allied lines in the Ardennes. The six American divisions holding the area fell back. General Eisenhower rushed in reinforcements and the 101st Airborne Division held the road junction at Bastogne. By the end of December the Allies had stopped the German advance, making the Battle of the Bulge one of the key battles of the war.

Antigone performed

ANTIGONE, BY FRENCH DRAMATIST Jean Anouilh, was first performed in 1944. It is based on a story from ancient Greece, but the characters wear modern dress. As the play was produced during the Occupation, French audiences identified the heroine, Antigone, with the Resistance and Creon with Vichy France.

Williams' *Glass Menagerie*

A PAINFUL FAMILY DRAMA set in St Louis was Tennessee Williams' new play published in 1944. *The Glass Menagerie* is about a mother's dreams of her glamorous past as a Southern belle, in sharp contrast to her present life. She persuades her son to supply a 'gentleman caller' for her crippled daughter.

The Razor's Edge published

W. SOMERSET MAUGHAM'S last important novel *The Razor's Edge* was published in 1944. It is a somewhat mystical story about an American hero who goes to India.

Grable and Crosby 'top'

THE MOTION PICTURE ALMANAC published a yearly poll showing the film stars who were 'tops' at the box office. These were the stars who earned most for American movie houses. Betty Grable was the top money-making woman of the movies for 1944, and the male winner was Bing Crosby. Both stars were leading attractions for much of the 1940s. Grable also won the poll for 1942, 1943, 1947 and 1949. Crosby also won for 1945, 1946, 1947 and 1948. (Other female winners in the 1940s were Bette Davis, Greer Garson and Ingrid Bergman. Other male winners of the decade were Mickey Rooney, Albert and Costello, and Bob Hope.)

Bacon's painting

FRANCIS BACON WAS AN ANGLO-IRISH ARTIST who used colour and blurred, featureless figures. His weird 'Three Studies for a Crucifixion' appeared in 1944 and made the painter famous. In 1949 he had his first one-man show in London.

The poet T.S. Eliot.

Oscar winners

THE ACADEMY OF MOTION PICTURE ARTS AND SCIENCES 'Oscar' winners for Best Actor and Best Actress in 1944 were Bing Crosby for *Going My Way* and Ingrid Bergman for *Gaslight*. Other award-winning films in the decade included *In Which We Serve, The Lost Weekend, The Best Years of Our Lives, Gentlemen's Agreement, Treasure of Sierra Madré, All the King's Men, To Each His Own* and *The Story of Bernadette*.

'Four Quartets' published

T.S. ELIOT'S MAJOR POEM 'The Four Quartets' was first published in 1944. It represents the four seasons and the four elements (earth, air, fire and water). In the first part of the poem the imagery is of a Cotswold garden. The second centres on a Somerset village, while the third mixes the landscapes of Missouri and New England in the USA. The fourth part uses the village of Little Gidding in Northamptonshire. The whole poem is concerned with time, past and present, including wartime London of the blitz. This was the first of Eliot's poems to be widely read.

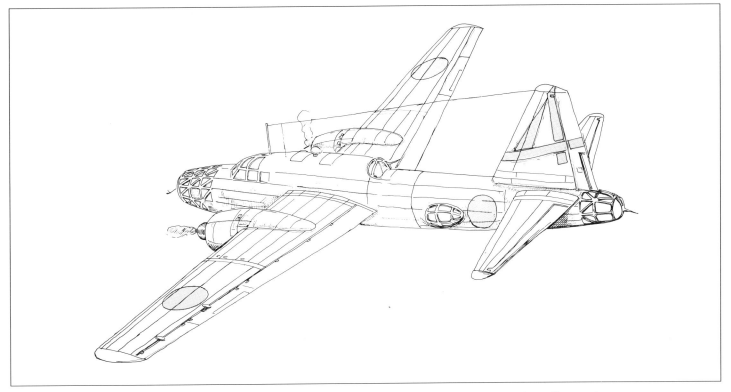

The Mitsubishi K-67 Hiryu heavy bomber entered service in 1944. It was the best all-around Japanese bomber of the Second World War.

DDT introduced

DDT (DICHLORO-DIPHENYL-TRICHLOR-OETHANE) was discovered in 1939 and introduced as an insecticide in 1944. Initially, it was regarded as a wonder product, helping farmers to kill off insect pests. Crop yields began to increase dramatically. DDT was used also to kill the mosquitoes that spread the disease malaria.

By the 1960s, however, there was growing concern about the side-effects of DDT, and it has now been banned in many countries. DDT is a poison that builds up in the body fat of animals and human beings. Besides health worries, there has been the problem of resistance. Many disease-carrying insects developed a resistance to the insecticide and were no longer controlled by DDT spraying. Modern efforts to control insect pests try to destroy the pests without harming other living things, including human beings.

DNA carries heredity

BY THE EARLY 1940s, the idea was developing that genes were part of a single chemical molecule, called Deoxyribonucleic Acid (DNA). It was soon established that every animal and plant species has a quantity of DNA in its cells. In 1944 DNA was shown to carry the characteristics that are passed on from one generation to the next. However, it was not until the 1950s that the details of DNA were known.

Chromatography

COMPLICATED CHEMICAL MIXTURES can be analysed by means of chromatography. For example, the mixtures giving beer or coffee flavour can be broken down into hundreds of components in just a matter of minutes.

The modern techniques evolved from the work of a Russian botanist Mikhail Tswett, in the early twentieth century. He separated the pigments or coloured materials found in plant leaves. Tswett coined the word 'chromatography' which means 'writing in colours'. This technique revolutionized chemistry after its usefulness was realized in the 1940s. Two British biochemists made important advances in 1944. They invented paper chromatography, which uses a paper strip instead of the crushed limestone used by Tswett.

1945

A-Bomb is

Fearful new weapon used

Hiroshima, Japan. The city was devastated by the atomic bomb.

ON 7 AUGUST 1945 the world's press reported that the Allies had dropped an atomic bomb on the Japanese port and army base of Hiroshima the day before. It was American President, Harry S. Truman, who decided to use the fearful weapon. (Truman had succeeded Roosevelt, who died in April of that year.) Truman's radio speech explained why he had taken the decision:

We have used it to shorten the agony of the war; to save the lives of thousands and thousands of young Americans. We shall continue to use it until we completely destroy Japan's power to make war. Only a Japanese surrender will stop us.

The one atomic bomb dropped on Hiroshima almost wiped out the city. Over three-quarters of its buildings were destroyed. Over half its inhabitants were killed or wounded. Some of the victims died immediately, while others died years later from the effects of radiation.

dropped

Eye-witness accounts

IN 1945 FUTABA KITAYAMA was a 33-year-old housewife. Her home was just 1.7 km from the centre of the blast. This is part of her account of what happened:

I don't remember which came first – the flash of light or the sound of an explosion that roared down to my belly. Anyhow, the next moment I was knocked down flat on the ground. Immediately things started falling down around my head and shoulders. I couldn't see anything; it seemed pitch dark. I managed to crawl out of the debris.

Soon I noticed that the air smelled terrible. Then I was shocked by the feeling that the skin of my face had come off. . . .

What had happened to the sky that had been such a clear blue only one moment ago? It was now dark, like dusk. I ran like mad towards the bridge, jumping over the piles of debris.

What I saw under the bridge was shocking: hundreds of people were squirming in the stream. I couldn't tell if they were men or women. They looked all alike. . . .

As far as I could see my declining eyesight was all in flames. . . . I saw on the street many victims being carried away by stretcher. Carts and trucks, heavily loaded with corpses and wounded who looked like beasts, came and passed me. On both sides of the street, many people were wandering about like sleepwalkers. . . .

Disarmament and World Development, Pergamon Press, 1978.

John Hersey, a New York journalist, went to the city in May 1946 to hear what happened:

A tremendous flash of light cut across the sky. Mr Tanimoto has a distinct recollection that it travelled from east to west, from the city towards the hills. It seemed a sheet of

Japan surrenders

THE JAPANESE DID NOT SURRENDER after Hiroshima, and so a second atomic bomb was dropped, on 9 August on the city of Nagasaki. This killed another 40,000 people. Finally, on 15 August, the Japanese Emperor, Hirohito, announced the unconditional surrender of Japan. The Second World War was over at last. 'Peace on Earth' was the *Daily Express* headline on 16 August.

Should the bombs have been dropped?

SOME PEOPLE HAVE SAID there was no need to drop the A-bombs on the Japanes cities. They said the Allies wanted to test the weapons. Truman and the Allies said the bombs were used to bring a quicker end to the war and so save lives. The awesome power of the new bomb stunned the world. As Truman said: 'It is an awful responsibility which has come to us.' No one knew how long term the effects of radiation would be, but it has since been held responsible for the rise in the rate of some cancers.

sun. Both he and Mr Matsuo reacted in terror, and both had time to react, for they were 3.2 km from the centre of the explosion.

Mr Tanimoto threw himself between two big rocks. He felt a sudden pressure and then splinters and pieces of board and fragments of tile fell on him. He heard no roar.

From the mound, Mr Tanimoto saw an astonishing panorama. As much of Hiroshima as he could see through the clouded air was giving off a thick, dreadful smell. Houses nearby were burning, and when huge drops of water the size of marbles began to fall, he half thought that they must be coming from the hoses of firemen. (They were actually drops of condensed moisture falling from the turbulent tower of dust, heat and fission fragments that had already risen miles into the sky above Hiroshima.)

Mr Tanimoto met hundreds and hundreds who were fleeing. The eyebrows of some were burnt off and slime hung from their faces and hands. Some were vomiting as they walked.

Under many houses, people screamed for help, but no one helped; in general, survivors that day assisted only their relatives or immediate neighbours. . . .

When Mr Tanimoto reached the park it was very crowded, and to distinguish the living from the dead was not easy, for most of the people lay still, with their eyes open. The hurt ones were quiet; no one wept, much less screamed in pain; no one complained: not even the children cried; very few people even spoke.

By nightfall, ten thousand victims of the explosion had invaded the Red Cross Hospital. Ceilings and partitions had fallen; plaster, dust and blood and vomit were everywhere. Patients were dying by the hundred, but there was nobody to carry away the corpses. . . .

John Hersey, *Hiroshima*, Penguin, 1946

Yalta Conference

PRESIDENT ROOSEVELT OF THE USA, Prime Minister Churchill of Britain and Joseph Stalin, leader of the USSR, met at a conference in February 1945. This was held at Yalta in the Crimea. A number of important problems were discussed.

The leaders and their ministers agreed on plans for Germany's defeat. Germany would be divided into four zones, to be occupied by Britain, the USA, the USSR and France. Frontiers for Poland were settled. The conference also discussed setting up the new United Nations organization.

"AND HOW ARE WE FEELING TO-DAY?"

Churchill, Roosevelt and Stalin met at Yalta on 4 February 1945 to try to cure the ills of the world.

Crowds in London celebrated VE-Day on 8 May 1945

The war ends

BY JANUARY 1945 Russian forces had reached Germany's eastern frontier. On the western front the Allies were preparing for a final campaign. Allied bombs caused much destruction when they raided Dresden in Germany.

The American army crossed the Rhine in March and had joined up with the Russians on the river Elbe by the end of April. On 24 April Russian troops entered Berlin and captured the city. Hitler committed suicide in his Berlin underground bunker on 30 April. German armies began surrendering in May, and on 8 May the war in Europe was finally over.

When Japan surrendered on 14 August the Second World War was finally over. Nearly 17 million fighting men had been killed, six million Jews had been murdered, and about 30 million other civilians had died from bombings, hunger, disease and other effects of the war.

The following are extracts from the front page of *The Daily Sketch*, 8 May 1945:

THIS IS VE-DAY
Premier is to Broadcast at 3 p.m.
Two Days Holiday
'An official announcement will be broadcast by the Prime Minister at three o'clock this afternoon. Today will be treated as Victory Day and will be regarded as a holiday. Tomorrow will also be a holiday. . . .'

WORLD MAKES WHOOPEE
All over the world the report of the German surrender was celebrated yesterday. Here is how the news was received as told in cables from all over the globe:
LONDON: Thousands flocked to town after the first pause of perplexity. Buckingham Palace and Piccadilly Circus were the converging points for thousands of revellers.
NEW YORK: Ticker tape and bits of torn-up telephone books fluttering down from skyscrapers proclaimed that the city was celebrating. Streets are knee-deep in paper, all telephones are dead and traffic diverted.
PARIS: Crowds cheered wildly outside a big newspaper office in a main Paris thoroughfare as loudspeakers announced the capitulation.
ROME: Sirens sounded in the city while church bells rang.
JOHANNESBURG: Flags and bunting went up. Newspaper sellers were mobbed by excited crowds.

New Labour government

IN THE EARLY SUMMER OF 1945 Britain's Conservative prime minister, Winston Churchill, dissolved the government. This had been a coalition, governing since 1940. The Parliament that was dissolved in 1945 had been elected ten years earlier with a strong Tory majority.

The result of the 1945 election was a landslide victory for the Labour Party. People hoped for better times. An election victory cartoon in the *Daily Herald* of 17 July 1945 showed a man, woman and child. They smiled as they climbed a hill into the sun. In the dark valley behind them were storms of 'slums', 'oppression', 'fascism' and 'fear'. The cartoon caption said 'Forward – and goodbye to all that!'

Labour's election programme, 'Let Us Face the Future', set out proposals for increased nationalization of industry and expansion of the 'welfare state' (a phrase coined in the 1930s). This meant an increase in the range of services offered by both central and local government to help with individual social problems.

Roosevelt dies

AMERICAN PRESIDENT, FRANKLIN D. ROOSEVELT, died on 12 August 1945. He was the only president to be elected four times. Roosevelt tried hard to keep America out of war ('Your boys will not be sent into any foreign wars' – election speech, 1940). By his Third Inaugural Address, on 20 January 1941, he and the nation knew they had to become involved:

We have learned that we cannot live alone, at peace; that our own well-being is dependent on the well-being of other nations, far away. We have learned that we must live as men, not as ostriches. . . . We have learned that we must be citizens of the world, members of the human community.

Potsdam Conference

AFTER PEACE FINALLY CAME, the post-war settlement had to be made. Churchill, Stalin, and Harry S. Truman, Roosevelt's successor, met at Potsdam outside Berlin from 17 July to 2 August 1945. (A new British Prime Minister, Clement Attlee, replaced Churchill in the middle of the talks.)

The Allied leaders managed to reach agreement on some issues. A Council of Foreign Ministers was established to work out peace treaties with Italy, Romania, Finland, Hungary and Bulgaria. The leaders also set up an international tribunal to try Nazi officials for their 'terrible crimes'.

War criminals stand trial

BEFORE THE WAR ENDED the Allies were already collecting evidence against leading Nazis. The first of a number of war crimes trials was held at Nuremburg on 20 November 1945. Among the 22 defendants was Hermann Goering, head of the German Luftwaffe.

Evidence at the trials showed films of concentration camps being liberated as well as official documents and eyewitness accounts. The horror of Nazi brutality was fully revealed. After a year, the tribunal sentenced some of the men to imprisonment and some to execution. Many leading Nazis were never found.

Sport and the Arts

Animal Farm published

ENGLISH WRITER GEORGE ORWELL published his novel *Animal Farm* in 1945. A satire on communism, it is about a group of animals who overthrow their human masters. One famous line from the book is 'All animals are equal, but some are more equal than others.'

Unité d'Habitation built

THE SWISS ARCHITECT Le Corbusier has had much influence on modern architecture. Many plans for modern tower blocks have been based on his ideas. In 1945, work began at Marseilles, France, on his tall building, Unité d'Habitation.

Le Corbusier specialized in low-cost housing and planning of flats on estates. He was concerned with the social problem of housing people in cities. Housing was seen as a 'machine for living in'. Unnecessary features were taken away, leaving a simple structure with flat roofs and plain walls.

Unité was Le Corbusier's answer to accommodating large numbers of people quickly and cheaply. The Unité in Marseilles has one large rectangular block carried on a double row of massive central supports. It contains 350 flats in eight double storeys. There is a storey for shops half-way up and communal facilities on the roof.

Jazz goes 'Bebop'

AMERICAN MUSICIANS PRODUCED a new form of jazz in the mid-1940s, called 'bebop'. Charlie Parker, a black alto-saxophonist, was the main creator. Young jazz musicians were breaking away from traditional harmonies. Parker, who became a jazz legend, explained his need to make music in a new way. 'Music is your own experience, your thoughts, your wisdom. If you don't like it, it won't come out of your horn.'

'Bird' by Miro

JOAN MIRÓ WAS A SPANISH PAINTER and sculptor. His 'Bird' cast in bronze was produced in the years 1944-6. In 1945 Miró began painting on large canvases and produced the first of a series 'Women and Birds'.

Peter Grimes first performed

ENGLISH COMPOSER Benjamin Britten's opera *Peter Grimes* was first performed in 1945. It is the most successful of all modern English operas. In his choice of subjects Britten showed his concern with cruelty and his sympathy for the 'outsider' in society.

The story is set in a Suffolk fishing village. Peter Grimes, a fisherman, has lost an apprentice at sea. Villagers are suspicious. Grimes is acquitted at the inquest and takes another apprentice. A schoolmistress discovers that the boy is being ill-treated and the village sets itself against Grimes. Peter and the apprentice try to avoid the mob as they

Ivan the Terrible, Part I

RUSSIAN FILM-MAKER Sergei Eisenstein began filming *Ivan the Terrible, Part I* in 1942. It is the story of Ivan IV (1530-84), the first Russian Czar, and has become a cinema classic. The film first opened in Moscow in 1945.

leave his cliff-top hut. As they are chased, the boy falls to his death down the cliff. A sea captain advises Grimes that to escape the village fury he must sail his boat out to sea and sink in it, which he does.

Charlie Parker, one of the leading jazz musicians of the 1940s.

Fluorescent lighting in Piccadilly Circus Station, London.

Arthur C. Clarke's plan

AN ARTICLE APPEARED in the periodical *Wireless World* in 1945 putting forward the idea of using artificial satellites as relays for radio and television. The article was by the British scientist and author Arthur C. Clarke. Clarke's plan attracted little attention at the time, but is now seen as a predictor of the future. The idea was to use 'geostationary' satellites. (If an artificial satellite is set up at a certain distance above the equator, it will remain directly above the same place as the earth rotates.) The idea of artificial satellites was still a dream in 1945, as was travel in space. It was another 17 years before Clarke's theory became a reality. The first transatlantic television link was made by satellite in 1962.

First fluorescent lighting

THE FIRST FLUORESCENT LIGHTS were installed in 1945, in the Underground station at Piccadilly Circus, London. A fluorescent lamp has a glass tube with two electrodes, a coating of powdered phosphor and a small amount of mercury. Light is produced by converting ultraviolet energy from a low-pressure mercury arc. It is phosphors that produce most of the light provided by a fluorescent lamp. Phosphors are chemicals that absorb radiant energy of a given wavelength and reradiate this at longer wavelengths.

Fluoridated water

THE FIRST COMMUNITY to fluoridate its water was the city of Grand Rapids, Michigan, USA, in 1945. Since the 1940s many communities have added fluoride to their water supplies, but this has been controversial.

Fluorine (chemical symbol F) is a gaseous chemical element first discovered in 1771. It is best known for its compounds, mainly sodium fluoride which helps prevent tooth decay. The enamel of teeth normally has some fluorine in it. If children drink water with one part per million of fluoride while their teeth are developing, their chances of tooth decay are reduced.

First General

General Assembly meets

THE FIRST UN GENERAL ASSEMBLY opened at Flushing Meadow, New York, on 23 October, 1946. American President Truman's speech included the following statement:

After the First World War the USA refused to join the League of Nations. This time the USA is not only a member, but the host to the United Nations. We are proud and grateful that the UN has chosen our country for its headquarters. This meeting of the Assembly symbolizes the abandonment by the USA of a policy of isolation. . . . People of every nation are sick of war. They know its agony and futility. . . . Another world war would shatter the hopes of mankind and completely destroy civilization as we know it. . . . The war has left many parts of the world in turmoil. . . .

World tries to unite

THE UNITED NATIONS took its name from the military alliance issued on 1 January 1942. 'The Declaration by United Nations' was signed by the United States, Britain, the Soviet Union and 23 other countries against Germany and Japan. What began as a war effort gradually became something more long term.

A League of Nations had been started after the First World War. This had little power or influence, largely because the USA did not join. By the end of the Second World War America was playing a leading role in creating the new United Nations.

The UN actually began on 26 June 1945 when 51 nations signed the charter in San Francisco. The world did not

Specialized agencies

BESIDES THE GENERAL ASSEMBLY, a number of specialized agencies were set up linked to the UN. The following began in the 1940s:

1945 Food and Agriculture Organization (FAO)
1945 International Monetary Fund (IMF)
1945 International Bank for Reconstruction and Development (IBRD)
1946 United Nations Children's Emergency Fund (UNICEF)
1946 UN Educational, Scientific and Cultural Organization (UNESCO)
1947 Economic Commission for Europe (ECE)
1947 Economic and Social Commission for Asia and the Pacific (ESCAP)
1947 International Civil Aviation Organization (ICAO)
1948 Economic Commission for Latin America and the Caribbean (ECLAC)
1948 General Agreement on Tariffs and Trade (GATT)
1948 World Health Organization (WHO)
1949 UN Relief and Works Agency for Palestine Refugees (UNRWA)

then see itself in a global way. There were few international organizations. Transport and communications did not yet make links between countries rapid. The setting up of the UN marked a new awareness among nations – awareness of the need to co-operate if mankind was to survive. The UN helped the world become a smaller, more interdependent place.

UN grows

SINCE THE START OF THE UN in the mid-1940s, over 80 new nations have been created. Areas that were once colonies of richer countries have become independent states.

The UN and its agencies began gathering information about the planet, living conditions and resources. These facts are used to try and help immediate problems, and to help plan for the future.

Through the UN, over 350 treaties and conventions have been accepted by member states. Some programmes give an early warning about disasters. The UN also runs world conferences and has 'years' and 'decades' on special topics. There are peace-keeping forces to help with disputes among member-states.

From just 51 nations in 1945, the UN has grown to include 159 countries of the world (98% of the earth's people). From just 12 specialized agencies in the 1940s, the UN had expanded to include 32 by the 1980s.

FAO famine warning

AN EMERGENCY MEETING of the UN's new Food and Agriculture Organization was held in Washington on 20-7 May 1946. The effects of war had left the world critically short of food. The Director General of FAO, Sir John Boyd Orr, warned:

Following the 1946 harvest, the world will be as badly off for food as it was at the time of the 1945 harvest.

Assembly of UN

He expected a world deficit of 450,000,000 bushels of wheat alone:

Even with a good harvest, there would not be enough to bring diets up to pre-war standards. The situation is grave. Famine is the greatest politician of all. Peace cannot be built on a foundation of empty stomachs.

The conference agreed to establish a 20-nation International Food Emergency Council to be guided by the FAO. There was a series of plans for allocating, conserving, distributing and producing food in the 1946-7 harvest time. There was to be a new 'world food intelligence service' to be run by FAO. The information gathered would be used by the new Emergency Council. The conference made a formal declaration of a 'united war against famine'.

A Conference of the new Food and Agriculture Organization, one of the UN's specialized agencies.

UNICEF begins

UNICEF WAS ONE OF THE SPECIALIZED AGENCIES created in 1946. As the International Children's Emergency Fund (ICEF) one of its first tasks was coping with the hardships still facing the world as a result of war. Within its first year, UNICEF was providing extra food for over 3,700,000 children (in China, Poland, Yugoslavia, Italy, Greece, Rumania, Austria, Bulgaria, Hungary, Czechoslovakia, France and Albania). A special report for ICEF on food shortages in Poland said that 'very bad nutritional deficiences' existed among the child population.

Bread rationing starts

IN BRITAIN THERE WAS POST-WAR rationing of some foods that hadn't been rationed during the war (e.g. potato rationing began in 1947). Bread rationing started in July 1946 and lasted until July 1948. This meant that bread, flour, cakes, scones and buns were on a new restricting scheme called 'Bread Units' (BUs for short). People of different ages were allowed different numbers of BUs a week. There was an extra ration for some groups of adults, such as manual workers. The BUs were needed to buy certain foods. For example, two BUs were needed to buy one small loaf of bread and three BUs were needed for one pound of flour.

Food ration books were still used in Britain after the war. Bread rationing began for the first time in 1946, and the average number of Calories eaten per person per day was about 2850 (compared to a British average of over 3300 in the early 1980s).

New Towns Act passed

BRITAIN'S NEW TOWNS ACT was passed in August 1946. The idea of building 'new towns' was to lessen crowding in major cities. Several new towns were built in the late 1940s: Stevenage (1946), Harlow (1947) and Peterlee (1948).

Britain was already a very urbanized country, though less so than today. About 80% of the population of Britain in the 1940s lived in towns and cities, as compared to over 90% in the 1980s.

National Insurance Act

A NEW NATIONAL INSURANCE ACT (1946) brought the whole British population into a complete welfare system. A fund was established and a Ministry of National Insurance set up. Employers and employees began making weekly contributions, and a new system of maternity grants, death grants and family allowances was organized.

Nationalization

AS PART OF ITS POST-WAR PROGRAMME, Britain's Labour government nationalized the Bank of England, the Coal Industry and Civil Aviation in 1946.

Exhibition at V & A

LONDON'S VICTORIA & ALBERT MUSEUM held a design exhibition in 1946 called 'Britain Can Make it'. This showed design at its best, but few of the products were actually available for general sale. The exhibition was nicknamed cynically 'Britain Can't Have It'. The demand for goods still far exceeded the supply.

British newspaper advertisement, 1946
Sorry to have to say "Wait for it". Short of manpower, short of material, the output of Slumberland Utility Mattresses is not meeting the demand. . . .

Bikini tests

AMERICAN NUCLEAR WEAPONS TESTS took place in 1946 on Bikini, part of the Marshall Islands in the South Pacific Ocean. (The very brief swimwear, which first appeared in 1947, was named after the site of the tests.)

Black equality

ON 3 JUNE 1946 THE AMERICAN SUPREME COURT announced that racial segregation (as allowed by law in ten states) was unlawful on buses crossing state borders. The Court ruled on a case of a 'Negro' girl who, when travelling in a bus going from Virginia to Maryland, had been arrested and fined $10 for refusing to change her seat and sit in the rear marked 'For Coloured Patrons'. (Such segregation was then common in trolley cars, buses and trains in the South.)

While the Supreme Court decision moved black equality forward, there were some set-backs as well. A Fair Employment Practices Committee (FEPC) had been set up by President Roosevelt in 1941 to see that no federal agency or company doing business with the government discriminated against whom it hired. The FEPC was disbanded on 30 June 1946. In its final report it stated that discriminatory practices in industry had been increasing since the end of the war. The FEPC gave a warning that 'this denial of equal opportunity . . . cannot fail to create civil discord.' Conflicts and struggles over the next few decades showed how right the FEPC warning had been.

One king stays, another goes

1946 WAS A MIXED YEAR FOR MONARCHS in southern Europe. In June Italina voters wanted a republic, and King Umberto II wa deposed. Meanwhile, Greeks approved of having a monarch and returned King George II to the throne.

Philippines independent

ON 4 JULY 1946 THE PHILIPPINE REPUBLIC declared its independence. America had administered the Philippines since 1898, and the islands had been under the rule of Spain for 300 years before that. There were ceremonies in Manila to mark independence and American General MacArthur spoke:

With this ceremony a new nation is born. . . . For 48 years our army has stood on these shores; its role has never been to rule, to subjugate or to oppress. . . . Let history record this event in flaming letters as depicting a new height of nobility in the relationships between two separate and distinct peoples of the earth. . . .

Berlin was very heavily damaged by bombing during the war. The Allies divided the city into sectors after the war, sharing control.

Churchill visits America

IN MARCH 1946 WINSTON CHURCHILL visited the United States and made a strong plea for Anglo-American co-operation. The Cold War tension between Russia and the Western powers was just starting to develop. He warned that 'an "Iron Curtain" has descended across the continent [of Europe].' In his famous speech at Fulton, Missouri, Churchill said:

Up to 1933, or even 1935, Germany might have been saved from the awful fate which has overtaken her, and we might all have been saved the miseries Hitler let loose upon mankind. . . . We must not let that happen again. . . . This can only be achieved by reaching . . . a good understanding on all points with Russia under the general authority of the United Nations Organization. . . .

Action painting

AN AMERICAN STYLE OF PAINTING called Abstract Expressionism began in the mid-1940s. Jackson Pollock was a leading figure in this. His technique was called 'Action painting', and his canvas 'Untitled' (1946) is an example. Paint was put on in a random way. Some was splashed, dripped or even just flicked on.

Pollock abandoned the conventional easel, brush and palette. He spread gigantic pieces of canvas on the floor and moved around in an energetic way. Pollock said he liked painting on the floor because he felt 'more at ease. I feel nearer, more a part of the painting, since in this way I can walk around it, work from the four sides and literally be *in* the painting.'

The popular press called Pollock 'Jack the Dripper' and his work helped make a revolution in art. 'Action painting' was more concerned with the *act* of painting than with any subject.

BBC resumes service

TELEVISION IN BRITAIN had only just started in the late 1930s and was shut down for the duration of war. Services were resumed on 7 June 1946 but grew only slowly. There were at first only two sessions of television daily: 3.00 p.m. to 4.30 p.m. and then 8.00 p.m. to 10.00 p.m. Licences bought in 1947 numbered fewer than 14,000.

At first, television could be seen only by those within a radius of 30 miles around London (because of limited transmitter power). By 1949 it was also received in the Midlands. (It was the early 1950s before most of the country was covered.)

An 'action painting' by Jackson Pollock. This one, 'Number 23', was painted in 1948.

Giacometti's figures

IT WAS JUST AFTER THE WAR that the Swiss-born artist Alberto Giacometti began his pencil-thin sculptures that made him world famous. The theme in his work is the isolation of man, and even groups show figures alone and apart from each other (e.g. 'City Square', 1949). Man endlessly struggles and man endlessly fails in the brutality of life. Giacometti himself once said 'All that I will be able to make will only be a pale image of what I see'. Giacometti's work reflected the existential philosophy being put forward by Satre and others at the time.

Iceman Cometh produced

EUGENE O'NEILL'S PLAY *The Iceman Cometh* was first produced in 1946. It is set in Harry Hope's saloon-hotel in New York in the early 1900s. The boisterous salesman Hickey tries to encourage down-and-outers in the saloon to go after their ambitions. He is arrested for murder and the others return to their dream world.

Spock's book

DR BENJAMIN SPOCK first published his manual, *Common Sense Book of Baby and Child Care*, in 1946. It was a best-seller and prompted a whole new approach to child-rearing. Stern methods were to be replaced with gentle understanding. Parents were encouraged to become 'friends' with their children.

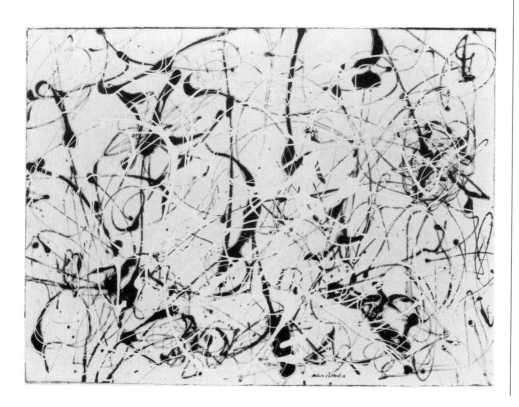

First electronic computer

THE FORERUNNER OF MODERN COMPUTERS was a machine designed by Charles Babbage in the 1830s. It was, however, the 1940s before electronic computers appeared. An ASCC, or Mark 1, machine was made in 1944 by a Harvard Professor together with IBM. This was a huge electromechanical calculator with about 3000 telephone relays. It was controlled by a punched paper table. The machine was over 50ft (15m) long and 8ft (2.4m) high. It took 0.3 seconds to add or subtract, four seconds to multiply and a full 12 seconds to divide.

The first electronic digital computer was completed at the University of Pennsylvania in 1946. Called ENIAC (Electronic Numerical Integrator and Calculator), it contained over 18,000 valves (vacuum tubes). These produced considerable heat, and faults were frequent. ENIAC could complete as much work in one hour as ASCC could do in a week. But changing programmes still took hours of manual rewiring.

In 1949, another important step came with EDSAC (Electronic Delay Storage Automatic Calculator). This was built at Cambridge. EDVAC (Electronic Discrete Variable Automatic Computer) was built at Pennsylvania. Instead of routing instructions through wires plugged into a perforated circuit board, stored programmes were used.

Electric blanket – with thermo switch

ELECTRIC ELEMENTS WERE BEING USED to heat beds as far back as the late 1800s. However, it was only after 1912 that electrically heated pads really began to sell. Some people who bought these sewed several together to make a larger pad. From this grew the idea of a whole electric blanket. The first commercially produced electric blankets were not made until the late 1930s, and it was 1946 before a blanket with a thermostatic switch was invented in the United States.

ENIAC (the Electronic Numeric Integrator and Calculator) contained 18,000 valves and 1500 relays. It was designed to calculate firing tables for the American army's artillery. It could work out a trajectory (flight path) in 30 seconds, as compared to the 20 hours needed without ENIAC.

Automated assembly

THE WORLD'S FIRST completely automated system of assembly began in 1946 at the Ford Motor Plant outside Detroit, Michigan. It produced one motor-car engine every 14 minutes, compared to the 21 hours it took to assemble an engine manually.

With an automated industrial process the machines carrying out the sequence of operations work automatically and also control themselves automatically as well. 'Feedback' on what is happening in the process is given back to the controlling mechanism. This 'feedback' is a key feature of any automated system. Automation in a manufacturing process may include the automatic transfer of components from one machine tool to the next.

1947 India

End of British rule

ON 15 AUGUST 1947, INDIA became independent and the new state of Pakistan was created. This ended nearly 130 years of British rule. Shortly before midnight on 14 August, the Indian Constituent Assembly convened in a special session in New Delhi. The President of the Assembly delivered his address in Hindi and in English. There followed a two-minute silence for those who had died in the struggle for freedom. Pandit Nehru, first prime minister of the Dominion of India, addressed the Assembly:

At the stroke of midnight, while the world sleeps, India will awake to life and freedom. Today we end a period of ill-fortune and India discovers herself again.

Colonialism had brought some benefits to India. A good system of railways and roads had been built. A unified postal and telegraph system began. Modern harbours were made. The framework for a modern judiciary system and civil service had been established. However, by the beginning of the twentieth century, a feeling of nationalism was spreading. The Indian National Congress had been founded in 1885. Originally, it wanted only a share in political power, but by the early 1900s the Congress party was asking for freedom and independence from British control and demands for 'Home Rule' increased.

Muslim–Hindu conflict

BRITAIN REALIZED she would have to give up her power, but the situation in India was difficult. One main problem was the conflict between the Hindu majority and Muslim minority. Muslims were in the majority in five provinces., Two of these provinces, Punjab and Bengal, were among the largest in India.

The Muslim League did not want to be a minority in a national state. Their leader was Mohammed Ali Jinnah, a lawyer who had been speaking out for independence. Jinnah called for a separate homeland for Muslims, including the provinces in which they were a majority. This would mean partition of the country. The Indian National Congress stood firmly for keeping India united. Between the years 1937 to 1947 debate about

partition was a major issue. During the Second World War various ideas were put forward for India's independence. Each idea faltered on the Hindu–Muslim difference over partition.

In 1945 the British established an interim government under Jawaharlal Nehru as a lead-up to independence. The Congress Party and Muslim League continued their opposition. Britain's Labour government then sent out Lord Mountbatten as Viceroy and Governor-General. His brief was to bring about some settlement between the two sides. Mountbatten felt the partition of the country was inevitable. Finally, the Congress Party also decided that the only way of settling the problem was to create a separate Muslim state.

Mahatma Gandhi

A KEY FIGURE in India's independence was Mahatma Gandhi. After being educated in India, he went to England in 1888 to study law. He came back to India in 1891 and practised as a lawyer. In 1893 he went to South Africa as a lawyer for an Indian firm. The Indian community there asked for his help against the discrimination they faced. In 1906 Gandhi began his first campaign of non-violent resistance. This meant disobeying laws, and he was imprisoned many times.

At the age of 45 Gandhi returned to India. He began an *ashram* (co-operative community) and helped peasants in various ways. His first hunger fast, to aid the cause of the poor, was in 1918.

At first, Gandhi was not against British rule in India. But during the First World War the British passed an Act restricting Indian freedoms. Gandhi planned a non-violent campaign against this in 1919. Thousands of Indians took part. Some protestors did turn to violence and the British reacted harshly. There was a massacre at Amritsar, when 379 Indians were murdered by machine-gun fire. This incident turned Gandhi against British rule.

In 1920 Gandhi encouraged a boycott against the enforced import of British cloth. Indians were urged to weave their own cloth on hand looms. Gandhi was imprisoned in 1922 but released in 1924. He was then made President of the Indian National Congress. In 1930, Gandhi led a protest against the British salt monopoly. He led a 320 km march to the sea. There he extracted salt, which was against British rules.

Gandhi went to London in 1931 for a

Independent

31 March 1947. Mahatma Gandhi talked with Viscount and Viscountess Mountbatten in Delhi. Mountbatten was then the Viceroy of India.

conference on India's future. He was imprisoned again in 1932 and began a fast. His protest was against the treatment of India's poor 'Untouchables'.

In 1942 the Congress Party passed a 'Quit India' resolution against the British. Gandhi was put in jail and released in May 1944. At the age of 78, in 1948, Gandhi began his last fast, to try and stop the riots between Hindus, Muslims and Sikhs that had followed independence. As Gandhi walked to prayer, he was shot and killed by an assassin.

Speaking of Gandhi, Pandit Nehru said:

The ambition of the greatest man of our generation has been to wipe every tear from every eye. That may be beyond us, but so long as there are tears and suffering, so long our work will not be over.

The princes

ANOTHER PROBLEM making independence difficult was the matter of the princes. For centuries, large areas of India were ruled by local princes, called Rajahs and Maharajahs. During the British colonial rule about 40% of India stayed under the princes' personal rule. Lord Mountbatten persuaded the princes to agree to the union and independence of the country. When India and Pakistan emerged as separate states in 1947, most of the princely states (except Hyderabad and Kashmir) agreed to Indian union.

Winds of change

THE INDEPENDENCE OF INDIA, Pakistan, Ceylon and Burma in 1947 was the beginning of the end of Britain's empire. Soon other colonies, in Africa and elsewhere, wanted independence as well.

World News

Princess Elizabeth married Lieutenant Philip Mountbatten RNA on 20 November 1947.

Princess Elizabeth marries

CROWDS FILLED CENTRAL LONDON to cheer Princess Elizabeth and Lieutenant Philip Mountbatten RNA on their wedding day, 20 November 1947. Thousands of people spent the night before camped in the Mall, London, to be sure of a good view.

Marshall Plan adopted

THE MARSHALL PLAN (also called the European Recovery Programme – ERP) was a programme of American economic aid to Europe after the war. On 5 June 1947 the American Secretary of State, George C. Marshall, put forward the idea in a speech. He spoke of the need for a programme of European economic self-help supported by America. The American Congress approved the idea in December of that year. The aid was to be administered by the American Economic Cooperation Administration (ECA) and the Organization for European Economic Cooperation (OEEC).

On 19 December 1947 President Truman spoke to the Congress and urged them to agree to ERP. Aid was to be partly in grants and partly in loans. The Cold War was just developing, and America was anxious to halt the conditions which they felt would aid the spread of communism. As President Truman said:

Our deepest concern with European recovery is that it is essential to the maintenance of the civilization in which the American way of life is rooted. . . . The next few years can determine whether the free countries of Europe will be able to preserve their heritage of freedom. If Europe fails to recover, the peoples of these countries might be driven to the philosophy of despair. . . . Such a turn of events would constitute a shattering blow to peace and stability in the world. It might well compel us to modify our own economic system and to forgo, for the sake of our own security, the enjoyment of many of our freedoms and privileges. It is for these reasons that the USA has so vital an interest in strengthening the belief of the people of Europe that freedom from fear and want will be achieved under free and democratic governments. . . .

George C. Marshall also summed up America's feeling, when speaking to the Senate Foreign Relations Committee:

Britain's hard winter of 1947 was all the worse because fuel was still in short supply. This train took 20 hours to travel from Wolverhampton to London.

Dead Sea scrolls found

ANCIENT MANUSCRIPTS WERE FOUND in a cave near the Dead Sea in 1947. When the scripts were examined it was found that they had belonged to Jews living at about the time of Christ. The scrolls have supplied important details about the origins of the Christian religion.

School-leaving age raised

THE AGE at which young people in Britain were allowed to stop their schooling was finally raised to 15 in 1947. The Education Act of 1936 had asked for this to happen in 1939, but it was postponed until 1945 and then delayed again.

to what had been consumed in 1946. Ministry of Fuel and Power advertisements explained that, because of the war, there was a shortage of generating plant. 'When all available generators are working, if people still continue to switch on fires and lights, then the only thing to do is to cut off supplies to some areas.'

GATT organized

A GENERAL AGREEMENT ON TARIFFS AND TRADE (GATT) was negotiated in 1947 among 23 countries. This is a mainly voluntary agreement for reducing the barriers to world trade. Virtually all important trading nations have now joined. (By 1980, 83 countries were full members and 33 nations were limited members.)

During the 1930s America had a policy of high tariffs. It was hoped that these would increase domestic production and employment. But it became clear that they were, in fact, slowing recovery, rather than helping. By the mid-1940s it was realized that an approach by a group of nations was needed. GATT has three main aspects: various tariff concessions; a code of principles and rules governing trade; and regular meetings for discussing and sorting out trade problems.

So long as hunger, poverty, desperation and resulting chaos threaten 270 million people in Western Europe, there will be steadily developing social unease and political confusions on every side. The vacuum created will be filled by the forces of which wars are made. . . .

Britain freezes – fuel short

IN 1947 BRITAIN faced its coldest winter since 1881. Shortages of fuel made the hardship worse. There were not enough miners. (One 1946 newspaper headline shouted 'MINES NEED 100,000 MEN'.) People had to find their own coal, using pickaxes, garden rakes, iron rods and shovels.

By May 1947 people were being asked to cut by a quarter the amount of gas and electricity they used, compared

Children needed on farms

A MESSAGE WAS SENT to British schools in 1947 by the Ministry of Agriculture and the Ministry of Education. At least 50,000 boys and girls were needed to help on the land that summer as well as during term-time.

Morrison announces exhibition

BRITISH MINISTER HERBERT MORRISON announced in December 1947 the idea for a national exhibition in 1951. This was to boost morale after all the hardships of the decade. Some thought it folly to use resources building for pleasure when materials were in short supply and needed for building homes and schools. Newspapers that month were still saying 'Christmas is not what it was', as shortages and restrictions continued.

New play by Williams

TENNESSEE WILLIAMS' PLAY *A Streetcar Named Desire*, was first performed in 1947. It tells of the disastrous visit of a neurotic woman to her married sister.

The play is set in America's Deep South, like many of Williams's other works.

Anne Frank diary published

AN AMAZING BOOK was published in 1947. In 1942 a 13-year-old girl in Holland was given a blank diary as a birthday present. She was still free but was already forced to wear the yellow six-pointed star which marked her as a Jew. Jews could not use a tram, go to the cinema, ride a bicycle. The restrictions were growing daily. Less than a month later the family went into hiding to avoid being rounded up by the Gestapo. The family hid in the upper back floors of an old building in Amsterdam. It was not until 4 August 1944 that they were discovered and taken to concentration camps. The girl, Anne Frank, and her sister, caught typhus and died in March 1945.

Anne Frank kept a diary during those years of hiding. It was later found and given to Dutch friends who kept it safe. Here are two extracts (Kitty is a make-believe friend to whom she wrote):

Friday, 21 August 1942
Dear Kitty,
The entrance to our hiding-place has now been properly concealed. Mr Kraler thought it would be better to put a bookcase in front of our door (because a lot of houses are being searched) but of course it had to be a movable bookcase that can open like a door. . . .

Monday, 3 April 1944
Dear Kitty,
Contrary to my usual custom, I will for once write more fully about food because it has become a very difficult and important matter, not only here in the 'Secret Annexe'. . . . The great attraction each week is a slice of liver sausage, and jam on dry bread. But we're still alive. . . .

The 'New Look', with its fuller, longer skirts and more feminine lines, was a big change in fashion.

'New Look' in fashion

IN 1947 A 'NEW LOOK' FASHION BEGAN, creating quite a stir. At the time, most women were dressed in square, angular 'man-tailored' clothes, with padded shoulders. Shoes were heavy, practical and masculine. Skirts were short and jackets long. In 1946 rules on clothes designing became less austere. As one newspaper columnist wrote: 'To the customer it means that the skimpy look in clothes will go'. The 'New Look' fashion that came in was much more feminine, with curved lines. 'New Look' skirts were very full.

Robinson joins Dodgers

JACKIE ROBINSON joined the American baseball team Brooklyn Dodgers in 1947. This made him the first black baseball player in the major league teams. Other Blacks followed and became some of America's greatest sports heroes.

Sportsman of the Year

THE DAILY EXPRESS 'Sportsman of the Year' award went to Cricketer Denis Compton.

Kon-Tiki expedition

THOR HEYERDAHL, a Nowegian scientist, and five companions set off on a scientific voyage in 1947. The goal was to sail from Peru across the Pacific Ocean to Polynesia on a raft made of locally grown balsa wood. The raft was called *Kon Tiki*. Heyerdahl believed that parts of Polynesian culture were like the culture of the ancient Peruvians. He thought the Polynesians might have come from South America, crossing the ocean on simple rafts.

Heyerdahl sailed for three and a half months, covering over 8000 km of ocean. He landed in Tuamotu Island in the South Pacific, showing that the voyage was possible. His book, *The Kon-Tiki Expedition*, was published in 1948.

Thor Heyerdahl's Kon-Tiki *expedition crossed the Pacific in 1947.*

'Flying saucers' spotted

IN 1947 AN AMERICAN PILOT reported seeing disc-like objects in the sky near Mt Rainier in Washington state. These objects came to be called 'flying saucers'. Since the late 1940s there has been much interest in the phenomenon of the UFO (unidentified flying object). Many bizarre and unexplained objects have been reported over the years. Speculation has been that these UFOs may be spacecraft from another planet. The objects are usually shaped like discs or cigars. Often they have bright lights and are able to hover and fly at high speeds.

Radiocarbon dating

THE PERFECTION OF RADIOCARBON DATING in 1947 has had great impact on archaeological research. Remains as old as 70,000 years have been accurately dated this way. The age of something with organic material is determined by the radiocarbon (^{14}C). Tests can be made on wood, charcoal, marine and fresh-water shells, bone and antler, peat and organic-bearing sediments.

Polaroid land camera

THE FIRST model of a polaroid camera was developed in 1947. A polaroid uses a diffusion-transfer process to give finished positive prints very quickly. The 1947 model produced brown positive prints in one minute. Later improvements made possible black and white prints in 10 seconds and colour prints in one minute.

Holography

THE BASIC PRINCIPLES of holography were first set in 1947 at the Imperial College of Science and Technology in London. (It was, however, the early 1960s before technology had advanced to make this a practical idea.)

Holography is a way of recording the information contained in the wavefront of light reflected from or transmitted by an object. It has attracted attention as a photographic technique in which lasers are used to record realistic images of three-dimensional objects. The photograph is called a hologram. When illuminated by a laser, the hologram produces images that are exact copies of the three-dimensional object.

Tubeless tyres

THE FIRST commercially successful tubeless tyres became available in 1947.

1948

New State

David Ben-Gurion, first Prime Minister of Israel, explained the Zionist cause.

New nation created

AT 4.00 P.M. ON 14 MAY 1948 the Jewish leader, David Ben-Gurion, made a radio announcement. The 650,000 Jews of Palestine listened as he said:

By virtue of the national and historic right of the Jewish people and the resolution . . . of the United Nations [We] hereby proclaim the establishment of the Jewish state in Palestine – to be called Israel.

A new nation was born, and with it tensions in the Middle East that have continued for decades.

Arab opposition

THE ARMIES OF FIVE ARAB NATIONS were gathered at Israel's borders, with Arab leaders saying they would throw the Jews into the sea. Israelis knew that their 40 million Arab neighbours did not want a Jewish state. After centuries of persecution, and especially after the

British rule ends

SOON BEFORE BEN-GURION announced the independence of Israel, British mandate in the Holy Land came to an end. The last British High Commissioner for Palestine took the salute for his troops and went by motor launch to a waiting cruiser. British rule had started during the First World War when, in December 1917, British troops marched into Jerusalem. Palestine was taken from Turkish control and a pledge was made by the British Foreign Secretary, Arthur Balfour. Called the Balfour Declaration, this pledge stated that

His Majesty's Government view with favour the establishment . . . of a national home for the Jewish people [and] nothing shall be done which may prejudice the civil and religious rights of existing non-Jewish communities in Palestine.

horrors of the Second World War, Jews regarded Israel as their homeland, a place of refuge in a hostile world.

Zionism

IN THE LATE 1890s, Jews in a number of countries began organizing a worldwide Zionist movement. This encouraged Jewish immigration to the Holy Land. By 1922 there were about 85,000 Jews living in Palestine amongst about 650,000 Arabs. Many of the Jews were refugees from anti-Semitic persecution in eastern Europe. Some were idealistic Zionists, who wanted a homeland for the Jews. Arab leaders were bitter about the way European powers were had assumed control of some Middle Eastern territory and they were upset at the growing size of the Jewish population. Anti-Jewish riots broke out in Palestine in 1920.

It was the 1930s before Jewish immigration really began to grow. The anti-Semitism of Germany's Nazi government drove hundreds of thousands of German Jews to settle in Palestine between 1933 and 1939.

# of Israel

British policy changes

EARLY IN 1939, Britain changed its policy on Palestine. War looked likely and the British government wanted to encourage Arab support. A white paper on Palestine was produced, limiting the number of immigrants to 75,000 over the following five years. (Over that time, millions of Jews were trapped in Nazi-controlled Europe, with millions dying in Hitler's concentration camps.)

The Zionists tried to save as many Jews as they could. Shiploads of Jewish refugees tried to reach the Holy Land. But few reached their destination. The British were determined to stop illegal Jewish immigrants and intercepted the refugee ships. Some were sent back to Europe; others were shipped to British-occupied territory in central Africa.

The uncaring policy of the British caused anger in Jewish Palestine. Even after the war, the British announced their policy on Jewish immigration would stay unchanged. Britain wanted Arab support, fearing the Soviets would gain control of the oil-rich Middle East. Palestinian Jews took up arms in defence against Arab raiders and also to attack the British in Palestine. In 1946 and 1947 there were assaults on the British garrison. Zionists smuggled arms and Jews into Palestine and aroused world opinion against British policy. Britain was being pressed by the Arab states not to soften her policy, by Jews to allow more immigration, and by American President Truman (who supported the Zionists). Finally, in 1947, Britain turned the problem over to the United Nations.

UN partitions Palestine

ON 29 NOVEMBER 1947 the UN General Assembly voted to partition Palestine into two independent states. There would be one state for the 1.1 million Arabs and one for the 650,000 Jews. For the survivors of Hitler's holocaust in Europe, this meant at least some refuge.

The Arabs were outraged at the partition. They attacked Jewish settlements and by December 1947 Palestine was in a state of civil war. Palestinian Jews raised some money for arms from Jews in America. Leaders of the surrounding Arab states sent invading forces into the Jewish sector. In the Arab-Israeli war of 1948-9, Israel won more territory. Most of the lands allotted to Palestine's Arabs were annexed by Jordan, and the Gaza Strip came under Egypt's control.

After the 1948 war about half a million Palestinian Arabs left Israel to live in neighbouring Arab states. Many ended up in refugee camps, where thousands still live today. The plight of these Arabs and continuing Arab opposition to Israel's existence have meant continuing unrest since the 1940s.

The Exodus *was one of a number of ships bringing Jewish immigrants to Palestine in 1947. Many immigrants on these ships were not allowed into Palestine and were taken to Cyprus for internment.*

World News

Apartheid declared

RACIAL SEPARATION was widely practised in South Africa before 1948, but it was in that year that the National Party extended the policy. 'Apartheid' is an Afrikaans word for 'apartness'. Dr Malan, the South African Prime Minister, outlined his government's apartheid policy to the House of Assemblies on 16 August 1948. This included separate schools for non-Europeans as soon as possible.

On that day, 16 August, there was an experiment in segregation on Cape suburban railways. Some first-class coaches were reserved for Europeans only. There was opposition, but this was made permanent on 12 September 1948.

An Electoral Laws Amendment Bill suggested that all Coloured applicants to vote should need to prove their qualifications before certain officials. Opponents said the government was trying to deprive Coloureds of their right to vote, as many non-whites would not be able to take time from their work to go before officials. The Bill was passed on 30 September 1948.

Apartheid meant a growing number of measures passed by the controlling white minority to restrict the majority Blacks and Coloureds. In a speech in 1948, Dr Verwoerd, Minister of Native Affairs, said:

The policy [of Apartheid] will aim at concentrating, in so far as is possible, the main . . . groups and sub-groups of Bantu in their own separate territories, where each group will be able to develop into a self-sufficient unit.

An Arab refugee camp for homeless Palestinians. The problem of displaced Palestinians became an issue over the next few decades.

OEEC formed

A CONVENTION WAS SIGNED in Paris in April 1948 by 16 countries: Austria, Belgium, Denmark, France, Britain, Greece, Iceland, the Republic of Ireland, Italy, Luxembourg, the Netherlands, Norway, Portugal, Sweden, Switzerland and Turkey. The British, American and French zones of Western Germany signed the convention as well. These countries set up the Organization for European Economic Cooperation (OEEC), with the aim of promoting economic growth and increasing trade. OEEC became the main organization for European Co-operation after the war. It was the forerunner of the European Economic Community (EEC).

Besides administering Marshall Plan aid, OEEC had other functions. Through its European Payments Union (EPU), OEEC organized a system of credits. This helped member nations to reduce restrictions on most of their trade with one another. OEEC also set up a system for regular discussion on matters of economic concern.

(The OEEC was replaced in 1960 by the Organization for Economic Cooperation and Development, OECD. This had a wider membership, including the United States. OECD became more concerned with Europe's economic links with the rest of the world.)

UNESCO reports

AT ITS SECOND GENERAL CONFERENCE, in 1948, UNESCO's Director-General reported on the UN agency's work in 1947. UNESCO had distributed over $100,000,000-worth of books, school materials, scientific and laboratory equipment to re-equip war-devastated countries. UNESCO had started many fellowships and travelling scholarships. It had helped to re-stock 2000 public libraries destroyed by war and had reconstructed museums in 13 nations. UNESCO also announced plans for a worldwide campaign against illiteracy.

National Health Service begins

BRITAIN'S NEW NATIONAL HEALTH SERVICE began in July 1948. The idea of a free, comprehensive health service had been part of Labour Party policy since 1934. An Act passed by Parliament in the autumn of 1946 nationalized the hospitals and general medical doctors.

Before the National Health Service began, about half of the nation's hospitals had belonged to local authorities. Standards of health care varied widely from place to place. Hospitals tended to charge patients according to their means.

In its first year, the new NHS treated over 8.5 million dental patients and supplied 5.25 million spectacles. There was a particular demand amongst poorer people, who had not gone for treatment previously because of the cost.

The National Health Service quickly became second only to the armed forces in the money and manpower it used. Because the service proved so costly, in 1949 the Minister of Health accepted the idea of charging for prescriptions.

Britain encourages immigrants

A BRITISH NATIONALITY ACT was passed in 1948 declaring Commonwealth citizens 'citizens of the UK and colonies'. As British passport-holders, these people had the right to come to Britain to live. The UK was desperately short of workers and *encouraged* immigrants to come. Factories, building sites, the new National Health Service – all needed more labour. (It was not until 1960 that restrictions started closing the door against immigrants.)

National Service act

BRITAIN'S NATIONAL SERVICE ACT (1948) required 18-year-olds to report for a compulsory two-year period of military service. The idea was that if war were to break out again Britain would have a larger number of trained young men ready to fight.

Stay-at-home Britain

A SURVEY by the British Tourist Holiday Board showed that only half of Britain's population spent its holidays away from home.

Alger Hiss took the stand to deny he was a member of the Communist Party.

Bacon ration down

IN NOVEMBER 1948 the bacon ration in Britain went down to two ounces per person per fortnight. The weekly food allowances were actually well below the averages during wartime.

HUAC investigates

IN 1948 the House Un-American Activities Committee (HUAC) began investigating charges against Alger Hiss, formerly of the State Department. A former Soviet agent said that Hiss had passed secrets to him. This Hiss trial prompted a public witch-hunt for 'communists' in America. This had become unreasonable hysteria by the early 1950s.

Sport and the Arts

Olympic Games

THE FIRST OLYMPIC GAMES since the war were held in Britain in 1948. It had been 40 years since Britain was host. The 1936 games had been held in Germany at a time when tensions were growing.

In the 1948 games America took 12 gold medals and Britain picked up four silver. Holland's four gold medals were all won by a woman runner, Fanny Blankers-Koen. She was one of the greatest female athletes of the twentieth century.

The most talked-about winner from the games was Emil Zatopek of Czechoslovakia, a distance runner who set a new record. His unusual way of sprinting prompted the comment 'He runs like an upright turtle'.

Television spreading

MAJOR OLYMPIC EVENTS were show on television, and, by the end of 1948, the number of licences held in Britain had reached 150,000. Some American programmes, such as 'I Married Joan' and 'Victory at Sea' were bought for showing in the UK. One British favourite was a magazine programme called 'Picture Page'. There was also Philip Harven, a television cook. 1948 was an important year for television in America. The comedian Milton Berle was very popular. New programmes started, such as Ed Sullivan's 'Toast of the Town' and Arthur Godfrey's 'Talent Scouts' (brought from radio).

T.S. Eliot wins Nobel Prize

THE NOBEL PRIZE FOR LITERATURE was won by Thomas Stearns (T.S.) Eliot. He was born in Missouri, USA, and later educated at Harvard, the Sorbonne and Oxford. He settled in England and became one of the century's most famous poets.

Novels published

AMERICAN NOVELIST NORMAN MAILER published his first novel in 1948. *The Naked and the Dead* was based on his experiences with the army in the Pacific.

South African writer Alan Paton published *Cry, The Beloved Country* as a plea for more understanding and co-operation between the races.

The Loved One by English novelist Evelyn Waugh appeared, following his successful *Brideshead Revisited*, which had been published in 1945.

English novelist Graham Greene published *The Heart of the Matter*, a story set in West Africa during the Second World War.

Then quickly, surreptitiously, as though he had no right to be there, he crossed to the window and closed it. There was a faint smell of face-powder in the room – it seemed to him the most memorable scent he had ever known. He stood again by the door taking the whole room in. . . . He had been instructed at home how to memorise, pick out the important details, collect the right evidence, but his employers had never taught him that he would find himself in a country so strange to him as this. . . .
The Heart of the Matter

ICA Founded

THE INSTITUTE OF CONTEMPORARY ART was founded in London in 1948, to promote artists of the time and their work.

The finals of the women's 80 metres hurdles at the 1948 Olympics. Fanny Blankers-Koen of Holland (far right) was the winner and a star performer at that year's events.

The highly successful British Morris Minor was launched in 1948. Petrol was still being rationed until May 1950.

Transistors

THE TRANSISTOR (a contraction of 'transfer-resistor') was invented in 1948, in the USA. This made possible the miniaturization of electronic equipment. Micro-circuitry led to the development of the modern computer.

For over 20 years, radio had depended on thermionic valves. The valve, or tube, was a glass bulb. It contained an anode and a cathode, which allowed it to amplify radio signals. Where complex circuits were used – in, for example, computers – large numbers of these valves were needed. A large amount of heat was given off. The earliest computers could be used for only about half an hour before burnt-out valves needed replacing. Early computers had to be quite large.

The invention of the transistor was announced in 1948 by the American Bell Telephone Company. The transistor had many advantages over the tube. It was much smaller, needed much less power and would last longer. A revolution in technology followed

Mount Palomar telescope installed

THE ROCKEFELLER FOUNDATION gave a grant in 1928 for the construction of a giant reflecting telescope. This grant went to the California Institute of Technology. The telescope, with a diameter of 200 inches (508 cm) was to be housed in an observatory on Mount Palomar in California.

A building and dome to support the telescope was built in 1938. It took another ten years to prepare the disc for the telescope's mirror. The finished mirror weighed nearly 15 tonnes. The completed telescope was finally installed in 1948.

from this. Small radios and pocket calculators became possible. Computers could also be made much smaller and were capable of doing much more. The silicon chip is a linkage of hundreds of transistors in one small unit.

Microwave ovens

THE FIRST MICROWAVE OVENS were made in 1948 by an American firm. Microwave cookers use energy from the electro-magnetic waves produced by a magnetron. The waves are similar to those which send radio messages. As the waves pass through the food their electro-magnetic energy is changed into heat. (Two Englishmen invented the magnetron in the early 1940s, but not with cooking in mind. It was meant to be used in radar beacons to help spot enemy planes more effectively.)

In conventional cookers, heat falls on the outside of food and moves into the food slowly. Microwaves act instantly *within* the food, and so cooking is much faster. Microwave ovens have been much improved since the 1940s' models. They are especially useful for quick thawing and cooking of deep-frozen foods, which normally need a long time to defrost.

WHO's vaccine campaign

THE NEW UN WORLD HEALTH ORGANIZATION announced in 1948 it would concentrate on tuberculosis, venereal disease, malaria and the death of mothers at childbirth as the 'priority ills of mankind'. A major campaign to vaccinate 15 million people against tuberculosis over the following 18 months was launched. WHO also announced its budget would be used for fellowships, teaching equipment and medical supplies.

Solar heating

THE FIRST HOUSE to be heated by solar power was built in America in 1948.

People's

Communists take power

A NEW PEOPLE'S REPUBLIC OF CHINA began on 1 October 1949. The Communists had spent years fighting for power, and they finally took control. Changes included reforms in how land was owned and worked. Much land owned by rich landlords was redistributed to poor peasants. Many people who resisted the revolution were reported to have been killed.

The Chinese Communist Party had been founded in Shanghai in 1921. In 1925, the Canton national government came under the control of Chiang Kaishek. A provisional national government was formed in 1927 and was soon recognized by foreign powers. Chiang Kaishek was President. He launched a series of campaigns against the Communists. By 1934, the Communists had been driven out of their main base and began what was called 'The Long March'. This took them over 6000 miles north to Shaanxi Province.

A full-scale invasion of China by Japan was underway by 1937. By late 1938 the Japanese army controlled the eastern provinces. It was not until 1945 that Japanese troops in China finally gave up. The armies of Chiang Kaishek, with the help of the USA, took the surrender of the Japanese and regained control of the territory. The Chinese Communists were still trying to win power as well. Civil war began in 1946.

By 1948 the Communists had gained control of nearly all of the north of China. They took Peking (Beijing) in early 1949. In May the *Daily Telegraph* reported:

Mao Tse-tung's 'People's Liberation Army' which entered Shanghai at 7.30 this morning had occupied practically the whole of the city tonight.

By the autumn, the Communist leader, Mao Tse-tung, proclaimed a People's Republic. The formal inauguration on 1 October was read before a crowd of 200,000 in the Square of the Gate of Heavenly Peace in Peking.

Republic in China

The CPPCC

A CHINESE PEOPLE'S POLITICAL CONSULTATIVE CONFERENCE (CPPCC) had the task of laying down the framework of the new republic. They adopted a 'Common Programme' of 60 Articles. In its preamble the 'Common Programme' declared that the victory had 'ended the rule of imperialism, feudalism and bureaucratic capitalism in China. From the status of the oppressed, the Chinese people has become the master of a new society.' One General Principle declared was that 'the feudal system which holds women in bondage would be abolished and that all women would enjoy equal rights with men in political, economic, cultural, educational and social life'. Articles 25-8 said that the 'State shall co-ordinate and regulate the State-owned economy.'

Mao Tse-tung proclaimed the foundation of the new People's Republic of China.

Mao Zedong (Mao Tse-tung)

THE MAN WHO LED THE CHINESE REVOLUTION and founded the new Republic was Mao Zedong. He was rebellious even as a young man. At the age of ten he ran away from school to escape the harsh beatings and discipline that were then part of school life. At 13 he was in direct conflict with his father. As Mao said, 'My father denounced me, calling me lazy and useless. This infuriated me. I cursed him and left the house.'

In the years 1908-11, there were severe food shortages in Mao's area. Mao's father was a well-to-do grain merchant. He continued to send his grain to the city while local people suffered. One of his father's grain shipments was seized by hungry villagers. Mao took their side against his own father. Mao's rebellion was becoming political.

In 1911, a revolutionary agent visited Mao's school. He denounced the Manchus (whose dynasty then ruled China) and called for a republic. Mao said, 'After hearing that speech, I determined to join the revolutionary army.'

Mao later worked as a librarian's assistant and joined a Marxist study group. 'In the winter of 1920, I re-organized workers politically for the first time and began to be guided by the influence of Marxist theory and the history of the Russian Revolution.'

In 1921, Mao went to Shanghai for the first meeting of the Chinese Communist Party. In 1922 he helped organize a strike by coal miners. In 1925, he was busy setting up peasant unions in the countryside.

From 1928 to 1934, Mao led a Jiangxi Soviet republic within rural south-central China. This gave him more experience in mobilizing peasants. When the Communist Party was forced to leave in 1934 he led 'The Long March' north. The Party relocated its base to the north-central part of China.

The Japanese invasion allowed Mao to strengthen his peasant army. With the victory of the Communist Party in 1949, Mao became head of the new People's Republic. He replied to objections that the government was more dictatorial than democratic by saying (1 July 1949):

The experience of several decades amassed by the Chinese peoples tells us to carry out the people's democratic dictatorship. That is, the right of reactionaries to voice their opinions must be abolished and only the people are allowed to have the right of voicing their opinions.

The country has gone through many upheavals and changes since the revolution of 1949. Strict controls by the state have had bad as well as good effects. Mao did succeed in bringing better security for the mass of Chinese peasants. The famines and extreme poverty of pre-revolutionary China became a thing of the past.

> Every Communist must grasp the truth: political power grows out of the barrel of a gun.
> Mao Zedong

China banned from UN

THE FORCES OF CHIANG KAISHEK fled to Formosa, which was renamed Taiwan. China had two governments. Britain recognized the new Communist government in 1950, but what was then a country of 300 million people was excluded from the United Nations. It was 1979 before full diplomatic relations were established between Communist China and the United States.

Berlin blockade lifted

THE CITY OF BERLIN lay in the German zone which the Russians occupied. However, Berlin itself was divided into four sectors after the war, each occupied by one of the three Allied powers or the USSR. In 1948 the Russians said the three Western Allies had no right to be in Berlin. Russia began blockading the city, cutting off links with the West. A massive airlift of supplies from Britain and America continued into Berlin. The Russian blockade was fully lifted in May 1949.

Children waited eagerly as planes brought supplies during the Berlin Airlift 1948-9. Two-and-a-half million West Berliners depended on the supplies from the United States and Britain.

NATO formed

IN APRIL 1949 – the North Atlantic Treaty Organization (NATO) was set up. The treaty was signed by the United States, along with 11 countries of western Europe. The countries pledged to help each other in case of attack. It was growing tension with the Soviet Union that prompted the NATO pact.

Iron and steel nationalized

IN 1949 BRITAIN'S LABOUR GOVERNMENT added iron and steel to the list of nationalized industries.

German Federal Republic established

IN APRIL 1949 the German Federal Republic became an independent sovereign state. Elections were held and the Christian Democratic Party, led by Konrad Adenauer, took office.

After Germany surrendered in 1945, the country was divided into four zones. As tension grew between the USSR and the three Allied powers, it became difficult to reunite all the zones as had been planned. In 1948 the three Western Allies, the United States, Britain and France, went ahead with plans for a democratic German government. This included only the zones which these Allies had occupied after the war. The Russian zone became a separate East German state.

Housing Act (1949)

BRITAIN'S HOUSING ACT (1949) began the idea of improvement grants to home owners by local authorities. These were meant to encourage more repairs and better maintenance of buildings. There was still a desperate shortage of homes because of all the damage caused during the war.

Clothes rationing ends

CLOTHING COUPONS were used for the last time in Britain in 1949. The rationing which began in wartime was finally ended.

Soviets explode bomb

STATEMENTS ISSUED ON 22 SEPTEMBER, 1949 by the American, British and Canadian governments announced that they had evidence that an atomic explosion had taken place in the Soviet Union. America was no longer the only nation with the atomic bomb. President Truman said in his statement:

Ever since atomic energy was first released by man, the eventual development of this force by other nations was to be expected . . . this recent development emphasizes once again . . . the necessity for a truly effective, enforceable international control of atomic energy which this Government and the large majority of the members of the UN support. . . .

Indonesia independent

INDONESIA BECAME AN INDEPENDENT sovereign state under a statute of transfer dated 27 December 1949. The formal transfer by the Netherlands to the United States of Indonesia ended 350 years of Dutch rule in the East Indies. Queen Juliana of Holland spoke at the ceremony, which came after four years of conflict between the Netherlands and Indonesia. She said:

Never before has it emerged more clearly how deep is the sympathy borne by the two nations towards each other. No longer do we stand partially opposed to one another. We have now taken our stations side by side, however much we may be bruised and torn. . .

Republic of Ireland formed

AT MIDNIGHT ON 17/18 APRIL 1949 the Republic of Ireland Act came into force. Eire became officially a separate Republic. The inauguration was marked by a 21-gun salute fired from O'Connell Bridge in Dublin and further celebrations.

Thousands of people watched the Irish tricolour raised over the General Post Office in O'Connell St. There was a march-past of the Irish Army and a fly-past of the Irish Air Force. Parades and special church services were held at centres outside the capital. The President, Mr Costello, spoke at a press conference:

We now stand alone, a nation on our own. . . . Small as we are, as a nation we have tremendous influence by reason of the fact that so many of our people are scattered over the Western world. . . . We can be of great assistance [in the world] if we can only get rid of partition, the last worry we have. . . . We hope that the cause of bitterness between North and South will be soon removed. . . .

While Southern Ireland became a Republic, Northern Ireland remained part of the UK. The difficulties of a divided Ireland grew rather than lessened over the next decades. In November 1948, when the Republic of Ireland Bill was discussed in the British House of Commons, Winston Churchill observed the problems:

Now that southern Ireland has separated itself altogether from the crown, the maintenance of the position of Northern Ireland becomes all the more obligatory upon us. . . . It is evident that a gulf is being opened, a ditch is being dug between Northern and Southern Ireland. . . .

Two Irish politicians, John Costello and Sean MacBride, explained why they wanted to break links between Eire and the Commonwealth.

Sport and the Arts

Ealing comedies success

EALING STUDIOS was a British production company which made films in the years 1931 to 1955. It was a series of brilliant comedies in the late 1940s that earned the Studios wide popularity. Three of the most famous (*Whisky Galore, Passport to Pimlico* and *Kind Hearts and Coronets*) appeared in 1949.

1984 published

GEORGE ORWELL'S last novel, *1984*, was published in 1949. The world is divided into three parts: Oceania, East Asia and Eurasia. Oceania is a nightmare society where the state has complete control over people's thoughts and lives. The hero is Winston Smith, who struggles hopelessly against totalitarianism. 'Doublethink' becomes the rule. Slogans chanted include 'War is peace', 'Freedom is Slavery', 'Ignorance is Strength'. In Orwell's nightmare vision, all must worship the head of the Party, Big Brother.

Do you begin to see, then, what kind of world we are creating? It is the exact opposite to the stupid hedonistic Utopias that the old reformers imagined. A world of fear and treachery and torment, a world of trampling and being trampled upon, a world which will grow not less but more merciless as it refines itself. Progress in our world will be progress towards more pain. The old civilisations claimed that they were founded on love or justice. Ours is founded upon hatred. In our world there will be no emotions except fear, rage, triumph and self-abasement. Everything else we shall destroy – everything. Already we are breaking down the habits of thought which have survived from before the Revolution. We have cut links between child and parent, and between man and man, and between man and woman. No one dares trust a wife or a child or a friend any longer. . . .

Faulkner wins Nobel Prize

THE 1949 NOBEL PRIZE FOR LITERATURE was won by William Faulkner. Born in the American southern state of Mississippi, his novels convey the world of the American South. One of his most famous books was *Intruder in the Dust*, published 1948.

Graham Sutherland's 1949 painting of author Somerset Maugham. Maugham was quoted in 1949 as saying 'I've always been interested in people but I've never liked them.'

Fry's play performed

ENGLISH PLAYWRIGHT Christopher Fry had his play *The Lady's Not for Burning* peformed for the first time in 1949. The drama is set in the Middle Ages.

Joe Louis retires

AMERICA'S LEGEND OF THE BOXING RING, Joe Louis, retired in 1949. He had become heavyweight champion of the world in 1937. Louis held the title for the next 12 years and defended it 25 times. He did return to the ring in 1950 for a few more fights.

Portsmouth victory again

PORTSMOUTH BECAME BRITAIN'S Football League Champions in 1949-50 for the second year in a row. (Liverpool had won in 1946-7 and Arsenal in 1947-8.)

Death of a Salesman

ARTHUR MILLER, American playwright, wrote several plays about the values of American life. *Death of a Salesman* was first performed in 1949. It tells of a man who thinks that happiness depends on success in business.

TV Westerns start

TELEVISION WESTERNS started in 1949 with the showing of Hopalong Cassidy films. Alistair Cooke wrote about the 'television craze' in 1949 saying:

Television is going to be part of our world. . . . We are doomed – or privileged, according to your point of view – to be the television generation.

Disposable nappies (diapers)

PARENTS WERE PLEASED as a new item, the disposable nappy, became available for the first time in 1949.

Building technology

STEEL WAS IN SHORT SUPPLY after the Second World War. Architects were turning more and more to using reinforced pre-stressed concrete. It was thought that the structural possibilities of concrete were virtually unlimited. Besides being inexpensive, concrete allowed a freedom of design which architects appreciated.

One great engineer of Europe who showed the possibilities of using concrete was the Italian Pier Luigi Nervi. He experimented in the 1940s with his idea of ferro concrete, in which he erected the metal-framed skeleton structures to support the cladding. The great roof of the Turin Exhibition Hall

The Turin Exhibition Hall in Italy was built with corrugated pre-cast concrete units.

(1949) is a main example of this.

The shortage of steel in post-war Italy encouraged Nervi to make use of reinforced concrete. The need for economies elsewhere also prompted building methods which saved time and cost. Pre-cast cladding in high-rise construction was one solution being tried.

A school made of concrete at Hunstanton in England, designed by Smithson, was one of the first works of what came to be called the 'New Brutalism' in the 1950s. The school was started in 1949 and completed five years later.

Time Chart

World News	Sport and the Arts	Science and Technology

1940

Germans invade Norway and Denmark.
(10 May) Germans invade Holland and Belgium.
(10 May) Winston Churchill becomes British PM.
(1-2 June) Evacuation at Dunkirk.
(June) Italy comes into war.
(June) Channel Islands occupied by Germans.
(15 September) 'Battle of Britain'.
(14 November) Raid on Coventry.

(April) The Council for the Encouragement of Music and the Arts (CEMA) launched.
For Whom the Bell Tolls published.
Film of *Rebecca* released.
'The Lady is a Tramp' is a hit song.

Plutonium (first artificial element) made.
Electron microscope appears.
First car with automatic transmission available.
Freeze-drying process for food discovered.
First Jeep designed.
First nylon stocking on sale.
Chain of early warning radar stations set up along south and east coasts of Britain.

1941

(11 March) US Lend-Lease Act provides aid.
(April) Germans invade Greece and Yugoslavia.
(27 May) German ship *Bismarck* sunk.
(June) Hitler announces invasion of Russia.
(August) Atlantic Charter signed.
(7 December) Japanese attack Pearl Harbour; US enters war.

'Leningrad Symphony' written.
The Last Tycoon novel published.
Watch on the Rhine play first performed.
Citizen Kane film released.

First British jet-propelled airplane flies.
Aerosol patented.
Chipboard first manufactured.
US Office of Scientific Research and Development (OSRD) created.
Terylene first produced.

1942

(January) Japanese invade Dutch East Indies.
(February) Japanese seize Singapore.
(March) Japanese conquer Burma.
(May) Battle of the Coral Sea.
(August) Germans attack Stalingrad.
(October) Germans and Italians driven out of North Africa by Montgomery: Battle of El Alamein.

L'Etranger novel published.
Blithe Spirit play produced.

First helicopter in manufactured production.
Launch of German V-2 rocket.
First controlled chain reaction of atomic energy.

1943

(February) Evacuation of Japanese forces from Guadalcanal
(April) Jewish uprising in Warsaw Ghetto.
Juan Peron comes to power in Argentina.
(July) Mussolini overthrown in Italy; new Italian government.
(November) US invades Gilbert Islands.

Frank Lloyd Wright starts design for Guggenheim Museum.
Kandinsky painting 'Circle and Square No. 716'.
'Wave' sculpture by Barbara Hepworth.
Fifth Symphony by Ralph Vaughan Williams.
Sartre's *L'Etre et le Neant* ("Being and Nothingness") published.
Oklahoma! musical opens on Broadway.

Modern ball-point pen patented.
First artificial kidney made.
Penicillin first produce on a large scale.

1944

Warsaw Rising.
(6 June) D-Day landing on Normandy beaches.
(June) VI flying bombs on Britain.
US GI Bill of Rights.
(20 July) Plot to kill Hitler fails.
(25 August) Liberation of Paris, then France.
(September) V2 rockets on Britain.
(December) Battle of the Bulge.

Antigone play first performed.
'Four Quartets' poem first published.
Glass Menagerie play published.
The Razor's Edge novel published.
'Three Studies for a Crucifixion' painting.

DDT introduced.
DNA shown to carry heredity characteristics.

Time Chart

World News	Sport and the Arts	Science and Technology

1945

(February) Yalta Conference.
(30 April) Hitler commits suicide.
(May) Germany surrenders.
(8 May) VE Day.
(26 June) United Nations Charter signed.
(July) IMF begins.
(July) IBRD begins.
(17 July to 2 August) Potsdam Conference.
(7 and 9 August) Atomic bombs dropped on Japan.
(August) UN FAO begins.
(14 August) Japan surrenders.
(15 August) VJ Day.

Animal Farm published.
Unité d'Habitation built in Marseilles.
Bebop jazz introduced.
'Bird' sculpture by Miro.
Ivan the Terrible film opens.
Peter Grimes opera first performed.
Brideshead Revisited novel published.

First fluorescent lighting.
First fluoridated water supply.

1946

(January) UNESCO started.
(4 July) Philippines independent.
(23 October) first UN General Assembly meets.
(December) UNICEF started.

Baby and Child Care published.
Hermann Hesse wins Nobel Prize.
The Iceman Cometh play first produced.
7 June: Television services resumed in Britain.

Nuclear weapons tests on Bikini Island.
First electronic computer.
First electric blanket with a thermostatic switch.
First automated system of assembly.

1947

(15 August) India becomes independent: new state of Pakistan created.
Dead Sea Scrolls found.
GATT negotiated.
(20 November) Princess Elizabeth marries.
(December) Marshall Plan adopted.
(December) Ceylon and Burma independent.

A Streetcar Named Desire play first performed.
The Diary of Anne Frank published.
'New Look' in fashion.

Kon-Tiki expedition.
Radiocarbon dating perfected.
Holography principles set up.
Polaroid camera developed.
First commercially successful tubeless tyres produced.

1948

House Un-American Activities Committee investigations.
(April) OEEC convention signed.
(14 May) State of Israel created.
(June) WHO established.
(July) National Health Service begins in Britain.
(July) British Nationality Act passed.
(September) Apartheid extended in South Africa.

Olympic Games held in Britain.
T.S. Eliot wins Nobel Prize for Literature.
The Naked and the Dead novel published.
Cry, the Beloved Country novel published.
The Heart of the Matter novel published.
The Loved One novel published.
Institute of Contemporary Art founded in London.

Transistor invented.
First house heated by solar power.
First microwave ovens made.

1949

(April) NATO formed.
(17/18 April) Republic of Ireland formed.
(May) German Federal Republic becomes independent sovereign state.
(May) Berlin blockade lifted.
(22 September) Soviets explode atomic bomb.
(10 October) People's Republic of China begins.
(27 December) Indonesia independent.

Death of a Salesman play first performed.
1984 published.
William Faulkner wins Nobel Prize for Literature.
The Lady's Not for Burning first performed.

Disposable nappies (diapers) first available.

Key leaders of the decade

Winston Churchill (1874-1965)

Winston Leonard Spencer Churchill was born the son of Lord Randolph Churchill and an American, Jennie Jerome. He entered the House of Commons as an MP at the age of 26 and held various government offices. Churchill became Prime Minister of Britain on 10 May 1940, the day that Hitler invaded Holland. He was already over age 65 but was seen as the kind of strong leader needed for the country.

Having led Britain through the war, he announced victory in 1945 and won the cheers of the nation. However, he lost the General Election as Britain elected Clement Atlee with an overwhelming majority. The country wanted social reforms. Churchill is remembered as one of the great leaders of the twentieth century.

Mahatma Gandhi (1869-1948)

As leader of the movement for independence in India, Gandhi earned the title 'Bapu' ('father') from the Indian people. They also gave him the name 'Mahatma' (meaning 'great soul'). Gandhi spent over 2300 days of his life in gaol for the causes in which he believed. Even after his death, Gandhi's ideas impressed the world. His methods of non-violent protest influenced movements worldwide.

Charles de Gaulle (1890-1970)

When France fell to the Germans in 1940 General de Gaulle fled to England to raise the standard of the 'Free French'. At the time of liberation in 1944, it was de Gaulle who led one of the first forces to enter Paris. He had much influence on French politics in the 1940s, and was elected first President of the Fifth Republic in 1958.

Hirohito (1901-   )

As emperor of Japan from 1926, his early reign was marked by rapid militarization. There were aggressive wars against China (1931-2 and 1937-45) as well as the attack on Pearl Harbour, which brought America into the Second World War. In 1946, a defeated Hirohito renounced most of his powers.

Adolf Hitler (1889-1945)

Adolf Hitler was born in Upper Austria, the son of a customs official who had changed his name from Schickelgruber. Adolf wanted to be an architect or painter but failed to gain admission to art school. He became a soldier and part of the German Workers' Party. This party changed its name to the National Socialist German Workers' Party in 1920, and Hitler became more and more interested in politics.

The world economic crisis helped to bring Hitler and national socialism to power against Poland and led the world into war. A fanatical leader, Hitler's policies included mass murder to try and create a German 'master race'. He committed suicide in 1945 as Germany's loss of the war was inevitable. His body was never found.

Mao Zedong (Mao Tse-tung) (1893-1976)

Mao Zedong led the Chinese revolution and founded the new People's Republic of China in 1949. He wanted social reforms to distribute wealth more equally. He also wanted to change China into a modern industrial state. In 1966 he instituted the Cultural Revolution. Mao continued as head of Communist China until his death in 1976.

Benito Mussolini (1883-1945)

Born the son of a blacksmith, Mussolini established himself as dictator of Italy in 1922. He dreamed of a new Roman empire and annexed Abyssinia in 1936 and Albania in 1939. In June 1941 he brought Italy into the Second World War, on the side of the Germans. In 1943 he resigned, was arrested and rescued by German parachutists. In April 1945 he and other fascists were caught by Italians, tried and then shot.

Franklin D. Roosevelt (1882-1945)

Franklin Delano Roosevelt, thirty-first president of the United States, had been struck by polio at the age of 39. Though confined to a wheelchair, he won the elections of 1932, 1936, 1940 and 1944. As President during the Depression of the 1930s, he put through a number of measures to help the problems of unemployment and poverty. This 'New Deal' included such projects as the Tennessee Valley Authority, which regenerated one of

Key leaders of the decade

America's poorest regions.

Roosevelt was reluctant to take America into the Second World War, but the Japanese attack on Pearl Harbour gave the US little choice. He led the war effort until his death in 1945, and was a key force in the creation of the United Nations.

Joseph Stalin (1879-1953)

Joseph Vissarionovich Stalin, Soviet premier, was the son of a cobbler. He became a professional revolutionary and helped Lenin and Trotsky plan the October Revolution of 1917. After Lenin's death, Stalin took power and began an ambitious Five Year Plan (1928-33), which resulted in near total centralization of the economy. It was also Stalin's decision in the late 1920s which enforced collectivization. Small peasant holdings were joined into collective farms.

During his 25 years as dictator, Stalin laid the basis for the modern Soviet state. He also led his country during the war against Germany. While a hero leader, he was feared, and many Russians died during his brutal 'purges' of 1936-8.

Harry S. Truman

Elected Vice-President of America in 1944, Truman became President in April 1945 on the death of Franklin Roosevelt. Truman was re-elected in 1948 in a surprise victory over Thomas E. Dewey. As the Cold War against Russia developed in the late 1940s, Truman led the anti-communist feeling.

Books for further reading

J.F. Aylett, *Links: Twentieth Century World History, Hitler's Germany*, Edward Arnold, 1987

Angus Calder, *The People's War*, Panther, 1971

E.R. Chamberlain, *Life in Wartime Britain*, Batsford, 1972

Basil Colier, *Japan at War*, Sidgwick & Jackson, 1975

Michael Denning, *Links: Twentieth Century World History, China 1900-49*, Edward Arnold, 1981

Constantine Fitzgibbon, *The Blitz*, Corgi, 1974

Nance Fyson, *Growing up in the Second World War*, Batsford, 1981

Nance Fyson, *Growing up in the Post-War Forties*, Batsford, 1985

Sarah Harris, *Finding Out About Fighting in World War II*, Batsford

Tom Harrison, *Living Through the Blitz*, Collins, 1976

C.A.R. Hills, *Living Through History: The Second World War*, Batsford, 1986

Vera Inber, *Leningrad Diary*, Hutchinson, 1971

Madeline Jones, *Finding Out About Life in Britain in World War II*, Batsford

Norman Longmate, *How We Lived Then*, Hutchinson, 1971

C.K. Macdonald, Blackwell History Project: *The Second World War*, Blackwell, 1984

Arthur Marwick, *British Society Since 1945*, Penguin, 1982

Colin Perry, *Boy in the Blitz*, Leo Cooper, 1973

Michael Scott-Baumann, *Links: Twentieth Century World History, Conflict in the Middle East*, Edward Arnold, 1987

M. Sissons and P. French, (eds.), *The Age of Austerity, 1945-1951*, Penguin, 1963

Studs Terkel, *The Good War*, (account of lives of Americans at home and abroad), Hamish Hamilton, 1985

Warren Tute, *The North African War*, Sidgwick & Jackson, 1976

A few general books on the twentieth century with material on the 1940s worldwide:

Trevor Cairns, *The Twentieth Century*, Cambridge University Press, 1983

Derek Heater, *Our World This Century*, Oxford University Press, 1982

John Ray and James Hagerty, *The Twentieth-Century World*, Hutchinson, 1986

Acknowledgments

The Author and Publishers would like to thank the following for permission to reproduce illustrations: The Architectural Press for page 65 (top and bottom); BBC Hulton Picture Library for the frontispiece and pages 6, 7, 12, 14, 16, 21, 25, 31, 34, 38 (bottom), 40, 41, 44, 45, 49, 50, 51, 54 (right), 56, 58 and 62; British/Israeli Public Affairs Committee for page 55; *Daily Express* for pages 5, 19 and 32; FAO for page 43; John Frost Historical Newspaper Service for pages 13, 30, 39 and 54 (left); Guggenheim Museum, New York, for page 22; Imperial War Museum for the colour poster on the front cover and for pages 3 (bottom) and 4 (top and bottom); National Film Archive for page 28; Photosource for pages 8, 9, 11, 15, 18, 20, 24, 26, 33, 36, 53, 57 and 60; Tate Gallery for pages 10, 46 and 64. The illustrations on pages 17, 23, 27, 29, 35, 52 and 59 were drawn by the Author.

Index

Numbers in **bold** refer to illustrations